THRIVING IN GOD'S WORD

A Year of Weekly Devotionals

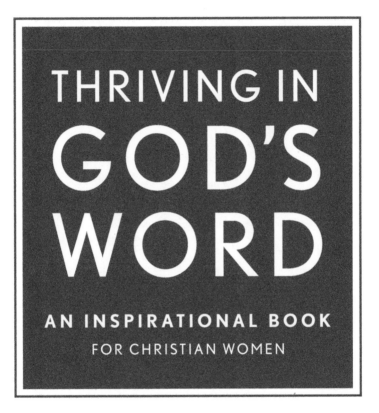

THRIVING IN GOD'S WORD

AN INSPIRATIONAL BOOK
FOR CHRISTIAN WOMEN

Christy Fitzwater

ROCKRIDGE
PRESS

Interior and Cover Designer: Jennifer Hsu
Art Producer: Karen Williams
Editor: Carolyn Abate
Illustrations by Creative Market/Vector Hut and Creative Market/BlackBird Foundry
Author photo courtesy of © Natalie Puls Photography

ISBN: Print 978-1-64611-939-4 | eBook 978-1-64611-940-0
R0

CONTENTS

INTRODUCTION

The winds are supposed to be howling today. Last night's weather report had a touch of humor to it. Our meteorologist included a "garbage can report." Would your garbage can remain upright? Or would it end up in your neighbor's yard? Maybe it would end up all the way down the street, as the newscast predicted.

It's not hard for my husband, Matt, and me to imagine a strong wind. Our bedroom is on the north corner of the house. A ski resort on the mountains north of us is easily visible from our backyard. On a clear day, you can see all the way into Canada. We get our wind straight from the province of Alberta, and when it hits, it feels like a semi has slammed into our bedroom wall, whistling through our windows. It's on those nights that we hope the builders of this house really knew what they were doing. The temperature in our bedroom is always a good five degrees colder than the rest of the house, too. Matt, who does not sport a head of hair, must wear a hat to bed in the winter.

Life can often feel like a north corner bedroom in Montana that constantly weathers the elements. I wake up sometimes and wonder if the garbage can will stand still today or some horrible wind of bad news or sickness or shame or trauma is going to send it flying down to the end of the street. Sometimes I feel my soul leaning into the pain of every day, and I wonder: If nothing bad happens today, will I just fall over?

Hard times slam against me like a wind straight out of Canada. Sometimes it's coming across a simple Facebook post that shows a dear friend saying, "My father went to be with the Lord tonight." Sometimes it's a broken faucet in the sink, and it will be $200 to buy a new one, thank you. And sometimes it's hearing a doctor use the word "disease" about someone I love. Gusts hit with no warning, but I have hope and a way to stand and thrive, even when the windsock blows straight. It's the hope of God's word, and I've found I can wrap my mind around his well-built framework of truth and stay upright.

I am a high school Spanish teacher and a pastor's wife, and during the course of my personal, professional, and church life, I have met with quite a few of these windstorms. What I'm offering to you in this book are stories of real, hard times that have happened in my life and how I grabbed onto Scripture truth and promises so that I didn't end up tipped over, blown into the neighbor's yard, or carried clear down the street.

The winds of hard times will come, because we live in a broken world. But we can stay upright and even live joyfully and with deep peace and hope. We can inwardly stand when the faucet breaks or the worst that we have imagined comes true. Peter tells the followers of Jesus they have what they need for life because of God's "exceeding great and precious promises" (2 Peter 1:4). Sometimes we feel like there's no way we could face another challenge, but we *do have what we need* to get through it. My hope is that as you read these devotions, thinking about the great promises and truths of God on each page, you will find that your feet stay on solid ground no matter what comes your way.

1

WILL YOU BE A VICTIM OR A DETERMINED STUDENT?

> *Get wisdom, get understanding.*
>
> PROVERBS 4:5A

On Monday I asked my freshmen students to draw a line down the edge of a big piece of paper and then write the number "10" at the top of the line and the number "1" at the bottom of the line.

"Now, I want you to think of the information that I hand to you on Monday of every week and that I test you on when Friday comes around," I said. "If 10 means you learn every bit of that information on a regular basis and 1 means you learn almost none of it, where would you say your learning lands?" I asked them to draw an arrow indicating what percentage of learning they felt they were accomplishing every week.

I then attempted a rousing speech about how the responsibility for that arrow belongs to the student. With a simple decision to learn more, each student could drastically change their own level of learning.

I explained that a few of my former students really struggled with Spanish. It was difficult for them. They had to work five times harder than most of the other students in the class to get the A's they were determined to get, but they persevered and succeeded. I then asked my students to write down three action steps that could raise the arrow of their own learning.

All great ideas, don't you think? That's what I thought until the Spirit of God became the teacher and I became the student. I'm currently in a difficult season of heavy responsibility, and please hear me say that with a flare of teenage whine to it.

This is the lecture that came to me from the Spirit: "Yes, this season is hard, but you get to choose whether you're going to whine your way through it or decide to learn and grow. Where will you draw your arrow?"

In Proverbs the command of Solomon is to get wisdom and understanding. The schoolteacher in me understands this command of "Learn!" But the schoolteacher in me also knows students have the freedom to choose—to learn very little or nothing at all. Every year I give my students pointers about how to succeed in my class, and every year many of them ignore me.

I don't want to be that kind of learner when it comes to following Jesus. I don't want to hear him say, "Don't be afraid," and then ignore him and live in fear. I don't want to read the wise command not to be anxious and then walk away only to continue living with anxiety. So, I draw my arrow at the 10. I believe this intense season of my life is an incredible opportunity to practice the information I've been reading in the Bible. I will not live in fear. I will not live in anxiety. My arrow is at the 10, and I *will* be an excellent learner, God help me.

JOURNAL: What is God trying to teach you right now? In the lines below, write a 1 on the top and a 10 on the bottom. Draw an arrow to show what kind of learner you're going to choose to be.

2

WHEN YOUR TO-DO LIST COLLIDES WITH GOD'S

A man's heart deviseth his way: but the LORD directeth his steps.

PROVERBS 16:9

My calendar was pretty simple until I added the role of women's ministry director to my life. Suddenly each month I had meetings several afternoons and evenings, plus phone calls to make and deadlines to meet. All of those dates were challenging to keep track of, so I needed a new plan. The administrators where I work use Google Calendar. Sure, I tend to sit on the edge of the technological pool, but was I brave enough to dive into the deep end and learn how to use Google Calendar for myself? (I'm 51 years old, so have pity on me.)

Once I figured out how to calendar meetings on my smartphone, I was in love. Google reminds me in the morning about what I have coming up for the day, and I get notifications right before events. Just the other day I had an important phone appointment and had forgotten about it. Thanks to Google, I had 10 minutes to gather my thoughts before the phone rang. Phew! I also like the feature that tells me of conflicts in my calendar so that there's no double booking.

However, the calendar app is lacking one big thing: It doesn't sync with God's appointments for me. Proverbs tells us that we may have our days all laid out, nice and organized on our calendars, but the Lord decides what we'll actually be doing on that day. Wouldn't it be so cool if there were a "sync with God's plans" app? Now that would be a hot seller!

I recently had a calendar-changing experience where I was laboring to get through the Christmas list of shopping, wrapping, baking, and packing for our family's holiday trip to Wyoming when a text came in from my friend who leads worship at our church: "Could you play the piano for the two early services on the Sunday I'm gone?" This is a friend who had been laying down her life to care for a very ill woman in our church. Was I really going to tell her "no" because I needed that time to finish baking Christmas cookies? The Lord was putting this opportunity in front of me, and it bumped everything on my list down a notch. I answered with a quick "I would love to!"

I won't lie; it hurt to give up precious hours on the very day I was supposed to be packing and leaving for vacation, but it was also a joy to be obedient to God. By the time we got in the car to drive away, I was exhausted from spending three hours at church in the morning and then racing around to finish packing, but I was also deeply happy. Sometimes it isn't a great deal of fun to let God rule my calendar, but it is very much worth it.

JOURNAL: Describe the last time you allowed God to interrupt your to-do list for the day. What was the result?

_____

_____

_____

_____

_____

_____

_____

_____

_____

_____

_____

_____

_____

_____

_____

_____

_____

_____

3

WHEN FOOD BECOMES AN ENEMY TO YOUR BODY

> *. . . life is more than meat.*
>
> **LUKE 12:23A**

A few years ago, in late November, our 25-year-old son-in-law, Dylan, started experiencing stomach pain that grew worse every day. He went to the doctor, who recommended he try a low-residue diet for a few weeks. During that time in December when we would gather together as a family and enjoy dinner, Dylan would only sit on the stairs, close to the dining room table, and sip a cup of broth and eat some JELL-O.

On Christmas Day, I called my daughter, Jayme, and she was in tears. Dylan could no longer stand up straight, because the stomach pain was so severe. She ended up taking him to the emergency room. By the next day, he had been diagnosed with Crohn's disease and ended up spending a week in the hospital.

I remember thinking my 24-year-old daughter shouldn't be sitting with her husband in a hospital room. She shouldn't have to be talking to doctors and nurses about medical tests and procedures. She shouldn't be hearing the word "disease" and trying to absorb the new lifestyle thrust upon them. But there we all were.

We mourned the health that Dylan had enjoyed just a month before. He began a special diet, and we learned how to cook new foods in special ways. Added to this daily expense of a new diet was the financial burden of hospital bills and new medication. There has been social pain with this disease, too. When we all get together now, Dylan can't eat the same foods everyone else is eating.

What do you do when someone you love is suffering and you aren't able to help? I was crying out to God in the night, asking him to heal Dylan if he so willed but also resigning myself to persevere through the trial if this proved to be our new normal. It has been a hard road.

The Lord brought me to one verse that gave me a comforting perspective. Jesus is talking to his disciples and encouraging them not to worry about what they will eat and wear. He says God takes care of the birds and makes sure they have food, and people are so much more valuable than birds. Then Jesus says life is about more than food and nourishment.

With the diagnosis of Crohn's disease, we all began to focus our energy on Dylan's food. But the verse was a good reminder that there is so much more to Dylan's life than what he was eating. It warmed my heart to read that God will take care of Dylan. We moms can cook special food, but it doesn't rest on my shoulders alone to make sure Dylan is okay. He has a Father in heaven who sees him and is taking care of him.

JOURNAL: Has food in any way taken center stage in your life? List some ways that being in the kingdom of God makes your life more than just about food.

_____

_____

_____

_____

_____

_____

_____

_____

_____

_____

_____

_____

_____

_____

_____

_____

_____

_____

_____

... count it all joy when ye fall into divers
temptations; knowing this, that the
trying of your faith worketh patience.
But let patience have her perfect work,
that ye may be perfect and entire,
wanting nothing.

JAMES 1:2-4

4

WHEN BOATLOADS OF RESPONSIBILITY HAVE YOU STRESSED OUT

I turned the calendar to the new year and then hyper-ventilated. On January 1, I began a new and daunting volunteer role at my church as women's ministry director. I signed the contract to author this book; I looked at my daughter's swollen belly and tried to imagine that in a few months I would become a grandma for the first time; and if that weren't enough, school was about to start back up.

All of these things coming at me were wonderful, but I couldn't breathe.

I had been quietly praying to be women's ministry director for seven years, and the Lord finally brought it to reality. My heart was filled with love for the women, and my mind raced with ways to help them know God and one another.

This book contract was a dream. Every devotion in this book is written with warmth and love for you, and I pray God will transform your life as you look at his word.

My daughter Jayme told me months before that the medicine her husband was on for Crohn's disease would make it very difficult for them to have a baby. When she announced she was having a baby, I cried tears of gratitude.

A lot of "new" was coming at me fast. On my way to bed one night, my chest and shoulders tight with stress, I said, "Lord, I can't do all of this. I just can't do it." That's when he brought the verses from James, quoted at the beginning of this devotional, to my mind.

That word *temptations* means "trials" or "proving." The Spirit made it clear to me that good and desirable things—those things we've longed for—can be a trial. Am I willing to say yes to what God is putting in front of me, even if it's stressful and means a lot of work?

Am I willing to admit my strength isn't going to be enough to manage all of this? Will I live in dependence on the Lord to provide what I need, in order to lead women and write and teach and love a grandchild? Will I choose to obey the command *not* to be afraid because God is with me, or will I live in constant fear of failure? Will I trust in the Lord with all of my heart, or will I try to do all of this on my own?

As I got ready for bed, I quoted the verses from memory, commanding my soul to do what they said: "Consider it joy! Consider it joy! You know this season that will require intense perseverance and faith in God will result in your maturity. Consider it joy, woman!"

The next morning, I woke up and said to myself, "Today is all you have. God just wants you to worry about today."

I spent time with Jesus, reading his word and praying. I sat down at the computer and stared at an intimidating blank page on the screen. Then I prayed: "Lord, I'm trusting you to give me words to share with women." And he gave me words! There's still a lot of work in front of me—in many directions—but I am considering it pure joy to dive into the work.

JOURNAL: What good but overwhelming tasks and responsibilities has God put in front of you to do? What has been your emotional response to these so far? Write a statement of joy and faith about these responsibilities.

5

WHEN BAD NEWS KEEPS COMING

> *Then Job arose, and rent his mantle, and shaved his head, and fell down upon the ground, and worshipped.*
>
> JOB 1:20

The text chimed while I was taking a breather at my desk for lunch. When I picked up the phone and glanced at the text, it was a kick to the gut. My cousin's baby didn't have a heartbeat. She was halfway through her pregnancy. I sat at my desk and sobbed. She had waited so many years to have a baby.

It had been two months of bad news. First was a friend whose husband was killed in a motorcycle accident. A little over one week later, another friend came home and found her husband dead with an empty EpiPen in his hand. Then it was a friend whose daughter up and left her husband

and family. Then there was another story of a friend whose spouse was unfaithful. The pain of hearing bad news layered on top of more bad news almost made me physically ill. I wondered if I could even pull it together to face my high school students.

In the book of Job, we hear about his experience of receiving a string of devastating news. One messenger came to tell him all of his cattle and oxen were gone, as well as the servants taking care of them. Then another message came that all of his sheep and the servants caring for them were gone. Immediately after that, he found out all of his camels and the servants caring for them were gone. Still another messenger came to say all of his children were dead.

I could understand the physical and mental impact all of this bad news had on Job's body, with no time to recover before the next hard thing hit. He must have been shaking and sick to his stomach. Job's response to this onslaught of bad news was to demonstrate his grief physically, by tearing his robe and shaving his head. Then he fell on the ground and worshipped God. In my distress, I became determined to copy him.

Kicking closed the door of my room, I laid my head down on the desk and physically let out the pain with my tears. I think I went through a half a box of Kleenex. After several minutes of inward wailing, I determined to worship God. It was exhausting, trying to steer my heart away from complete despair and choosing to praise the Lord instead, but worship was cool water over the heat of suffering within me.

JOURNAL: What sorrows have come at you in succession lately? What are two or three characteristics of God for which you will praise him today?

6

PUSHING BACK THE DARKNESS OF THE SOUL

Ye are the light of the world.

MATTHEW 5:14

We live in the town of Kalispell in Montana. It's one hour south of the Canadian border. From our house, we can see an entire range of the Rocky Mountains, ending with a view into Glacier National Park. It's breathtaking, and over two million visitors come through our town per year.

Us locals like to call our town "cloudy-spell," because we average about 150 days of sun per year. Since we are situated on the west side of the Rockies, our weather favors the wet, overcast days you might imagine for Washington or Oregon. On top of that, we're so far north that in the middle of winter our days are very short. My students start their day before the sun is up and by the time 5 p.m. rolls around, night is upon us.

As you can imagine, winter in Kalispell can be dark, even during the day. It's not uncommon for people to feel depressed during this time of year in Kalispell. Recently I was reading something about Finland, where they have even shorter days than we do. The writer explained that the people don't complain about it. They just cozy up in their houses and enjoy winter.

It's hard for me to imagine folks in Kalispell *not* complaining about the short, dark days of winter. I couldn't get Finland out of my mind. I thought about the flameless candles and lanterns my mom had given me. I use them for Christmas, but what if I were to make them a part of our winter joy? When she asked if I wanted several more I said an enthusiastic "Yes!"

After Christmas, I kept out the candles, setting some in the kitchen, in the living room, in the bathroom, and in several windows. My husband, Matt—a sun lover and one of the unhappy winter souls—loved the light. I really enjoyed the cozy evenings and brought it up often. After all, it's in my power to infuse enjoyment into our situation and to draw attention to where there *is* light.

This brings me to our greater situation: There's no question we live in a dark world right now. Even in broad daylight the news often feels like bleak midwinter—a never-ending cloud cover of cancer diagnoses, school shootings, drug addiction, broken families, and corruption. During these bleak times, it's more important than ever to remember Jesus looks at his followers and tells us we are the light of the world. He tells us we are the flameless candles that cozy up any corner and make it seem soft, warm, and inviting, even when outside is pitch black.

We must embrace the light. We have to decide we've had enough of letting the darkness get us down. But how? Spend time with Jesus and our Bibles. Go to church and sing songs of praise. Pray and pray and pray. Become internal sun lovers until we glow and the people around us start to think, "Maybe there's some hope in this world after all."

JOURNAL: What news has you feeling depressed or hopeless right now? Write down three truths about Jesus that feel like candlelight on a dark day.

7

PARENTING ADULT CHILDREN THROUGH UNCERTAIN SITUATIONS

> *I am Alpha and Omega, the beginning and the end, the first and the last.*
>
> **REVELATION 22:13**

During our normal FaceTime with our son, Caleb, and his wife of one year, Mallory, he casually announced that the next day would be his last day of work. My husband and I listened in stunned silence as he explained that his employer had lost one of its biggest clients, the one that paid Caleb's salary. Our son had his normal happy-go-lucky response. He wasn't worried. Instead he had already submitted job applications to no fewer than 25 different companies.

Caleb shared with us some of the job possibilities. One of them would allow him to be much more social and creative than his previous job did. I promptly said to God that

I thought this job just had to be *it*, and I got my hopes up. Hopes are good.

But what if he didn't get it? Would he have to work another job he didn't enjoy? Would the next job pay well enough to cover their budget? And when would they know?

Worry, at its best, is a mom's responsibility, right? Moms just want to fix things, like when Caleb was little. He'd forget his lunch, and I would bring it to school. I always put new clothes in his closet during his growth spurts. If I saw a problem, I took care of it. Parenting adult children means it's no longer my role to step in to repair or manage the hard things. It's my job now to listen, care, and lift my son in prayer to the God whose role it *is*.

To sooth my anxiety over Caleb's job hunting, I turned my mind to worship the Lord. The verse quoted at the beginning of this devotional came to mind. God is the beginning and the end. God exists now and to the very end of things, which means he exists in my son's future. We can only think forward and hope for things to go the way we want them to for Caleb, but God already knows clearly, in Caleb's specific future, what steps he wants my son to take and what is good for him.

In my prayers, I decide, over and over again, that God loves my son more than I do. I'm a good mom, but God is Good, with a capital G. My vision is limited to right now, but God already exists all the way to the end of Caleb's story. This kind of trust has required me to pry my fingers loose from the mom grip of control. Worry and a panicky need for control slip away when I bow at the throne of the Alpha and Omega.

JOURNAL: Whom do you tend to worry about and to control in your life? How does it help you relax your grip to know God exists in that person's future?

_____

_____

_____

_____

_____

_____

_____

_____

_____

_____

_____

_____

_____

_____

_____

_____

_____

See then that ye walk circumspectly, not as fools, but as wise, redeeming the time, because the days are evil.

EPHESIANS 5:15-16

8

LIVING WITH INSOMNIA

It's been more than two decades now since I first experienced insomnia. Normally I go to sleep just fine, but around 2 or 3 a.m., I wake up. In the early years of experiencing insomnia, I would weep and thrash about, trying to go back to sleep. Eventually I learned that if I got up and moved around, my mind and body would settle, and I could go back to sleep.

Even though I'm a professional insomniac, I've learned that I can foolishly wallow in the torment of not sleeping, adding to my own misery, or I can wisely redeem the time, as the apostle Paul instructed in the verse at the start of this devotional. *Redeem* means to buy up something for one's own use, so I do that. I buy the awake time and make it work in my favor.

When I first wake up, I lie in bed and pray my way through everything that is weighing on my mind. I meditate on Scripture I have memorized to quickly ease any anxiety. I also worship God, which causes him to come into my view as big and powerful, and all of my worries seem much smaller.

Once I have prayed, I get up and set up the coffee pot for Matt so that when he wakes up in the morning, he can just hit the start button. The physical routine of measuring and pouring grounds into the coffee filter, filling the water reservoir, and setting out his favorite coffee thermos helps my mind go to a simpler place. The love and affection I feel for Matt edges out the brain overload that wakes me up in the night.

Sometimes, if there's something on my to-do list that I can quickly take care of, I do it. One night I sorted the stack of paperwork that littered my desk. A few minutes of organizing helped my brain feel less chaotic. Sometimes I'll send out a few emails. People are always laughing and asking if I really sent something at 3:47 a.m. They think I'm crazy, but taking care of a bit of business clears my panicky feeling that I can't get everything done. Other times I turn to inspiring or encouraging books and read for a little while.

When I finally slip back into bed, I submit my sleep to God. I always say, "Lord, only you can cause me to sleep, so would you help me? And if you don't, I will accept that from your hand and trust you'll give me strength to get through the day." I turn back to prayer, meditation, and worship. Sometimes it takes a while, but I almost always can go back to sleep and wake up feeling rested.

Insomnia can lead to either a waste of time or time we redeem to become something useful. We can do small tasks, perform acts of love for our family while they're sleeping, and experience quiet, uninterrupted time for prayer and worshipping the Lord.

JOURNAL: What is your normal response if you can't sleep in the night? List some things you could do if you can't sleep, to buy that time for your own good use.

9

HAVING HARD CONVERSATIONS

> *And be ye kind one to another . . .*
>
> EPHESIANS 4:32

In my first year as a high school Spanish teacher, I was a coward. No one warned me about the strong minds and voices of teenagers. Standing before them, I trembled. At the same time, I had concerns about behavior and learning difficulties. I knew I needed to have difficult private conversations with students, but my churning stomach begged me to protect myself from such a terrifying prospect.

I also had to talk to parents about some hard topics regarding their children, and that prospect was even more terrifying. My imagination worked fabulously, creating scenarios of how horribly those conversations would go and how I would be hated and lose my job.

A friend at church, whom I respected very much for his leadership ability, said to me in passing one day that it's important to learn how to confront people. I did not like that idea at all. For a coward like me, confronting people about difficult topics seemed impossible. It didn't help that my principal believed confrontation was awesome. One time, after I told him about trouble that I was having with a student, he said, "Talk to the student and then call his parents. Let me know how it goes." Let him know how it goes? So, he was actually expecting me to do both of those things? I wanted to throw up.

But I did it. What I quickly found out was that it helped to have those hard conversations. In fact, the more I talked to the students and parents, the more I learned about the real struggles that families were enduring. Often parents would give me insight into the problems so that I could serve their child better. Parents were happy I had contacted them, and my relationship with students deepened. I learned that confrontation is a good thing—rather than misery—and that it's an act of kindness. The other option is to ignore problems and let them grow, which I now perceive as an act of cruelty.

Paul writes to the followers of Jesus in Ephesians and tells them to be kind to one another, and that believers are supposed to forgive each other, but how can forgiveness happen without offense and necessary confrontation?

I still hate confronting people. I don't think the task will ever be comfortable for me, but now I see the value and the kindness of caring about someone enough to talk about the unpleasant topics. I've changed my mindset to consider hard talks to be one of the greatest acts of kindness I can do for the people I truly care about.

JOURNAL: Describe a time in your life when someone confronted you about something hard, and you're so thankful they did. Is there anyone in your life right now who could use the kindness of a difficult conversation?

10

GOING UP AGAINST YOUR OWN BAD HABITS

> *. . . be ye transformed by the renewing of your mind . . .*
>
> **ROMANS 12:2**

"In 2020, I am going to love to exercise!" I announced with gusto to my family over the Christmas holidays. They kind of gave me a sideways look.

"In 2020, I am going to love to exercise. It's going to be awesome!" I announced again a day later.

"Is that some kind of New Year's goal?" my brother asked.

"No, I'm just talking myself into what I want to be next year," I said. He raised an eyebrow like I was a little crazy. He might not be wrong.

I believe myself to be an intelligent person. I know exercise is necessary for healthy muscles and bones and a healthy heart. I know getting my heart pumping helps me stay fit and maybe in the same size jeans. I know it helps prevent diabetes. I know it improves mental alertness.

But I don't exercise, because I don't want to. I want to read books and bake cookies and putter around the house. I want to see what exciting photos are posted on Instagram. I want to write blog posts and work on school lesson plans—even fold laundry. But I do not want to put on tennis shoes and give up 30 minutes of my life to get on a treadmill or, even worse, go outside and take a walk in the Montana cold.

I started my own pep talk campaign, which meant loudly proclaiming, for all to hear, that I was going to *love* exercise in the next year. I grabbed my phone and made a different calendar reminder for myself every day.

- Monday: Don't let yourself go, woman!

- Tuesday: Fifteen minutes matter.

- Wednesday: Get your blood flowing to your brain!

- Thursday: Be a fit old person!

- Friday: Sore muscles feel good!

- Saturday: Strong muscles. Strong bones.

- Sunday: Start with tennis shoes.

My intelligence about the health benefits of exercise doesn't equal the stubbornness within my own mind about not wanting to make the effort. But God has given me a brain that can either stay conformed to a self-serving, sedentary lifestyle or be transformed by ploughing new ways of thinking into it. Instead of the normal "I hate exercise. I don't want to put on my tennis shoes. I would rather do anything else" mantra that I've always told myself, I'm practicing speaking more positive words that sound like the kind of language someone who values exercise would actually say to herself.

It helps to remember how God has already transformed my life by changing the way I think. I used to hate cooking dinner and felt like a failure in the kitchen until God helped me change the way I was thinking about preparing food for my family. Now I love making dinner for my family, because I learned to think differently about this old habit.

I know God can change the whole exercise thing for me, too. Even though I'm 51 years old, Scripture tells me old dogs can learn new tricks. So, I'm running towards transformation by thinking in-shape thoughts and saying them out loud. I want this body to be a well-maintained, reliable vessel for God to use in his kingdom work.

On New Year's Day, my adorable little niece, who had heard my loud exclamations about exercise during the whole week of Christmas, asked if she could call me. During our call she said, "Aunt Christy, did you love exercising today?"

"I did, Emma! I got on the treadmill, and I did love it!" I told her.

This was the beginning of another life transformation.

What is one area of your life where you're intelligent enough to know you should live better? What new thoughts do you need God to help you plough into your brain for you to experience transformation?

_____

_____

_____

_____

_____

_____

_____

_____

_____

_____

_____

_____

_____

_____

11

GOD IS PRESENT WHEN YOU NEED HIM

> *God is our refuge and strength, a very present help in trouble.*
>
> **PSALM 46:1**

The moving-out deadline was days away, and we still faced an impossible amount of packing and cleaning to do. But I knew that in the last-minute crunch, my husband, Matt, was going to swoop in and do the majority of the heavy work. My endless weeks of daily packing, painting, and cleaning were about to wind down.

Except Matt came down with influenza. I could see him flagging as he tried to help me. When I finally told him to go to his mother's, he went there and stayed in bed for the next several days.

No problem; I was only beyond exhausted and alone. My first emotional stop was to have quite a lovely pity party. Why couldn't God have chosen another time for the flu to visit our family? I mean, why did I have to do the end sprint by myself? There may have been tears.

But I quickly came to my senses. I was definitely not alone. Exhausted and discouraged, yes, but not alone. I began to pray and get practical. "Okay, Lord. It's you and me," I prayed. "I am going to need everything you've got to help me get through these next hours and days by myself."

That afternoon I put in hours on the house, deep cleaning the master bathroom and packing along the way. It was grueling, but God gave me a crazy amount of energy, obviously from his own supply because I had been D-O-N-E. My initial prayer for help turned into hours of conversation as I removed the calcium build-up from the shower doors. It turned out to be an intimate, lovely time with the Lord that I could not have imagined possible earlier that afternoon. I even felt joy. I mean, this had to be God, because *no one* feels joy when they're praying for Lime-A-Way to do its work.

A few days later I went to a baby shower at church. A woman asked me how moving was going, and I teared up a little when I told her Matt had come down with the flu. She and her daughter's eyes lit up, and they asked what they could do to help. My pride almost kicked in, except the Spirit whispered in my ear, "Umm, remember you asked me to help you. Tell them what you need." So, I asked for help.

They were true to their word—fresh, energetic, and happy workers. The mom packed up drawers, while the daughter cleaned the kitchen counters and cabinet shelves to within an inch of their lives. They were new to our church family, so while they worked I got to hear all about their story. Their help came with a relational blessing. What sweet friends these two women have become in my life since then.

These women are part of a large hard-working rancher family. On our final day they showed up en masse to finish the job and move our remaining posessions into storage. When Matt had the flu and all seemed hopeless, God swept in for the rescue. It makes me cry just telling you about it.

JOURNAL: What impossible situation are you facing right now? Write a prayer asking God for help, and then "hide and watch," as my dad would always say.

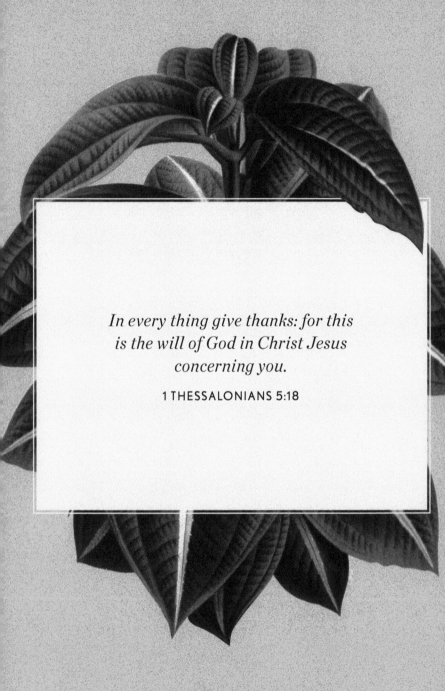

In every thing give thanks: for this is the will of God in Christ Jesus concerning you.

1 THESSALONIANS 5:18

12

FACING MONDAY MORNING WITH A NEW PERSPECTIVE

"I'm sorry you have to do Monday morning," Matt said to me as he watched me gather my purse and bag full of teaching supplies to head into another week as a high school teacher. I grunted in agreement. Mondays are hard. I've found it's much easier *not* to go to work.

But when I headed to the car, the Lord brought to my mind the memory of a young man I had met during summer vacation. We were at my mom's house for the Fourth of July, and her friends from Alaska were visiting and brought their 19-year-old grandson, who had cerebral palsy. They were his caregivers.

This young man could not walk. He could not speak, only grunting and moaning sounds. He could not control the muscles of his body—his arms and head moved in involuntary jerks. When it was time to eat, I watched the grandparents feed this young man and wipe his chin.

When I got to school, I continued thinking about this man. I was immediately filled with gratitude that I was able to walk out the door of my house and go to work. I could drive a car. I could go to the bathroom by myself and eat lunch without any help. I decided I needed to share this gratitude with my class, so I turned to them and told them about my experience with him.

"Even if you're not doing very well in my Spanish class right now," I said to them, "I want you to be grateful that God has given you the ability to learn a language and speak with others. And you have the physical ability to learn new words and communicate in a second language."

It's hard being a teacher. The interactions in one school day are many and unpredictable. There's a lot of opportunity for error. Sometimes the thought of it all wears me out—hence the tendency to give in to Monday morning blahs.

That day I decided doing hard work, even with challenges and sometimes failure sprinkled throughout, is a blessing from God. How dare I walk into a new day with a grumbling attitude? So, I am choosing to enter Monday mornings with an overwhelming gratitude to God for all that I am able to do.

JOURNAL: What is your normal attitude at the beginning of your work week? Write a prayer of gratitude, specifically thanking God for the tasks you have the privilege of accomplishing on a Monday.

13

WHEN YOU NEED
EMOTIONAL SHELTER

> *For ye are dead, and your life is hid with*
> *Christ in God.*
>
> COLOSSIANS 3:3

At the end of a regular faculty meeting, we did the normal encouragement time that the principal had instituted earlier in the year. People were encouraged to stand and read a word of praise to another teacher—a kudo for something they had seen that teacher do—and hand the teacher the handwritten card of encouragement. It was always special to hear teachers point out ways they had seen their colleagues shine.

Except no one ever said anything about me. Ever.

Before you think poorly of my colleagues, allow me to reason with you. I am a part-time teacher who comes to school midmorning, teaches a few classes, and goes home before the school day is over. My room is far away from all of the high school rooms. I rarely cross paths with the other high school teachers, and they certainly haven't seen me in action. It makes sense that no one could praise me for my work, because they've never seen me work.

Being passed over for praise happened during several meetings, and it never bothered me until the day it did. One day I felt small and insignificant—on the outside of the circle looking in. It hurt. Self-pity started to suck me in, an inward shrinking, but then I remembered the verse from the opening of this devotional. Since I am a follower of Jesus, my life is now safely tucked away in a secret place with Christ in God. I had read a poem called "The Little Gate to God" by Walter Rauschenbusch, who describes this hidden life in which we can mentally slip through a little back gate and be in God's presence.

I decided to practice living in the truth. For just a moment, I mentally slipped away from the faculty meeting and imagined myself going through the little gate into the throne room of God. I looked to God in prayer and asked, "Lord, what do you think of me?"

The Lord answered by bringing to mind his Son who had died to demonstrate his love for me. "I love you. You are my child," he whispered to my heart. My heart filled with the joy of being noticed and loved. This took less than one minute. I then mentally returned to the meeting, and everything was changed. I no longer felt insignificant. I no longer had that groping-heart need to hear the men and women in the meeting giving me praise.

Since that day, I have made it a habit to slip away to my hidden place in Christ. In him I find every word I need to hear and every resource I need for life.

JOURNAL: Describe the day when you died to yourself and found new life in Jesus. Now describe a time when you mentally slipped away to the hidden place with him and came away satisfied.

14

WORRY ISN'T HELPING YOU AT ALL

> *Which of you by taking thought can add one cubit unto his stature?*
>
> MATTHEW 6:27

My son Caleb was getting married in Houston, Texas, just a few days after Christmas. As I mentioned before, we live in the uppermost west corner of Montana, so we needed plane tickets for my husband, son, daughter, son-in-law, and me. I also had to reserve an Airbnb for eight people and find a rental car. I spent weeks thinking through all of the logistical details and making plans for the trip.

Buying the plane tickets raised my blood pressure. I was worried about buying the wrong dates, and we'd all show up a day after the wedding. What if I put down the wrong identification information on someone's ticket, and they couldn't get on the plane because their name didn't match their ID? What if I reserved the Airbnb on the wrong dates or lost the code to get through the gate and into the door? I also had to reserve a restaurant for the rehearsal dinner, sight unseen. I imagined walking in and the hostess telling me we didn't have one.

Oh, and the weather—you can't blame me for this worry. We had to fly to Houston by way of Denver, which is known for its weather closures. I lost a lot of sleep imagining us sleeping on the floor of the Denver airport. And let's not forget the luggage. What if the groomsmen's ties ended up in a lost suitcase?

Thankfully, we made it to Houston, luggage intact, including all of the groomsmen's ties. The Airbnb was lovely, and the rehearsal dinner at the restaurant went off without a hitch.

The day before the rehearsal we went to our new in-laws' house for dinner. This was our first time meeting them. We ate tacos with handmade tortillas from a local taqueria and enjoyed a warm and friendly dinner. The whole trip was as wonderful as planned, until we hit the pig.

Yes, you read that correctly.

We were driving on a dark country road in our rental car when a feral hog ran in front of us. There was no missing him. We struck him with the front bumper and felt him go under the front tire and then the back tire. Pulling over, my husband and son-in-law got out and reported that the front bumper of the rental car was cracked.

It was not fun to tell that to the rental company, although I laughed when the guy on the phone said,

"Oh, the poor pig," before he asked if we were okay. Even funnier is the fact that I worried about everything in the world—the weather, luggage, plane tickets, rehearsal dinner, and Airbnb—but I didn't worry about a pig. Jesus says worrying adds nothing to our lives, so why do it? Now I know worrying is a waste of time and energy, because I don't even know what I should actually worry about.

JOURNAL: What are you worrying about these days? How is this worry robbing from your life instead of adding something to it?

15

WHAT WILL YOU DO WITH UNFAIRNESS?

> *. . . and him that taketh away thy cloke forbid not to take thy coat also.*
>
> LUKE 6:29B

We thought she was going to be a really great tenant—a single mom with two kids—but it didn't turn out that way. We got our first complaint from the homeowners' association (HOA) that her kids were wandering unattended through the neighborhood, knocking on people's doors and asking to come in. We communicated a gentle reprimand through our property manager. When I had to bring something to the renter one day, I discovered two big dogs who were not approved under the lease.

A month or so later, I again saw the phone number of the HOA president show up on my caller ID. Our neighbors were upset because our tenant's dogs were coming into their yard. Again, I communicated a reprimand through the property manager. Some months later the rent came late. The following month, half of the rent arrived late. The subsequent month, no rent at all.

I knew this young mom was going through a painful divorce, and my heart went out to her. We overlooked a lot of issues, but we couldn't financially afford to let our tenant float, because the rent was paying our mortgage. Matt and I discussed our predicament. On one side of the conversation was her contractual and financial obligation. On the other side was a struggling young mom. It wasn't hard for us to understand the financial impact for her. What to do?

Thankfully, our tenant decided to move. It was Christmas, and we forgave the unpaid rent for the last two months and let her out of the lease with no penalty.

Within a few weeks, we had new renters in the house, and we discovered the previous renter's dogs had completely ruined the carpet. We paid close to $4,000 to have the entire house recarpeted. At one point, the thought came to me that we could sue this woman and try to get our money back. But Jesus said to me, "Has she taken your rent money? You might as well release her from paying for the carpet, as well."

The whole thing was unfair, but we were able to be the kindness of Jesus to the young mom last Christmas.

JOURNAL: Who has been grossly unfair to you, and what have they taken or done? Describe specifically what it would look like if you were to return their unfairness with generosity.

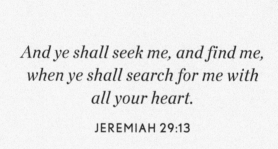

*And ye shall seek me, and find me,
when ye shall search for me with
all your heart.*

JEREMIAH 29:13

16

THE STRUGGLE TO KNOW AN INVISIBLE GOD

It was the most natural act for me as an eight-year-old, to decide to call Jesus the Lord of my life. I had been to church three times a week since birth and had heard the good news of forgiveness and the welcome door into the kingdom of God more times than I could count. I told my mom I was ready. She sat down next to me on the bed and listened to me pray the words of confessing my belief in Jesus as the Son of God and calling him the Lord of my life.

That was in May. In midsummer, one sunny day after church, our entire congregation drove down to the Popo Agie River where I was to be baptized. Down into the frigid Wyoming waters I went. Up I came, as a symbol of walking in newness of life with Jesus, and with a slight case of hypothermia.

Mom wrapped a towel around me, the church family congratulated me on my demonstration of faith, and with chattering teeth I went back to the car to get warm. On my way there, I felt profound disappointment. I was wet. I was cold. But where was God? I felt nothing, and I thought I should feel his presence.

The day of my baptism began an eight-year journey of questioning and doubting and wondering where God was. Why couldn't I feel him inside of me? I felt anxious at church, like maybe I truly hadn't been welcomed into God's kingdom after all. Maybe I had messed up, or maybe the whole thing wasn't real. Though I was young, I experienced a dark, desperate groping for God.

I remember specifically one day in high school biology class, as my mind wandered from cell division, I reached out in hunger again for God: "Lord, if you're really there, I just want to feel you. I believe in you with my head, but my heart feels empty. Where are you? How can I know you?"

That following summer, I went to a church camp. We had a choice of breakout sessions in the afternoon, and I chose one about how to have "quiet time." I sat on the grass on a warm day and learned practical tools for how to spend time daily with God—how to pray, memorize Bible verses, and study my Bible. I took notes and came home from camp eager to try the quiet time thing.

So, I did. The first time felt awkward and seemed like forever—the clock said it had been three minutes. But every day I kept spending time with God in prayer and Bible reading, again and again. One day God specifically answered a prayer and a flicker of hope lit in my heart. God had heard me! The more I spent time with him, the more I experienced the very real and vibrant presence of God in my heart. One day I realized I *felt* God within me, not just in my head but deep in my heart. The doubt was gone.

I searched for the invisible God with all of my heart, and I found him.

JOURNAL: How would you describe your experience with God? If you are still searching to know him in a real way, write a prayer telling him of that desire.

17

THE DISAPPOINTMENT OF SPECIAL DAYS NOT BEING SPECIAL

> *God is our refuge and strength, a very present help in trouble.*
>
> **PSALM 46:1**

My last birthday started off with a night interrupted by tossing and turning, so on my birthday morning I was tired—not just from a previous long day and a lack of sleep, but also from several weeks packed with more taxing activity than I'm used to doing. I just wanted to sit under a quilt, sip coffee, and read all morning.

But there was work to be done. I needed to tidy up my office before I started into the work week. There was also laundry to fold and my normal Sunday cleaning of the kitchen.

Matt took me for a birthday lunch, but I had to push down feeling overwhelmed. We had a nice time, but it was a short window of fun in a long day. That afternoon, I sat down with a red pen and a stack of freshman Spanish tests in my lap. I pouted for having to grade papers on my birthday.

Later that evening, my extended family came over for a birthday dinner. I was trying hard to be warm and social, but this felt like work. I started to feel guilty, because what kind of person would perceive family as work? Soon everyone left except my daughter and son-in-law, and I felt like a birthday spoiler, yawning my way to bedtime and unable to work up any decent conversation.

On Monday morning, my name was on the birthday board in the school office, so everyone kept saying, "Happy birthday. Did you have a wonderful day yesterday?"

Did I have a wonderful day? I was loved by my family, but really it was a long, hard day for the most part. But I talked to God on my birthday. I chatted with him while I was cleaning the kitchen. I asked for perseverance to grade papers. I begged him to help me stay awake and be sociable with my family.

What is it we expect from birthdays, Mother's Day, Valentine's Day, and other holidays? We set ourselves up for disappointment, when we think one day on the calendar is going to be all kinds of perfect, including our emotions. It's possible, however, to have a very good day, if we know life is going to be its normal level of difficult and we have God as a refuge in the middle of it. Having a place to go to for help and knowing that we're never alone is what brings a touch of warm sunshine to the day.

JOURNAL: When was the last holiday when you felt disappointment because the day was hard? Write down any ways in which you experienced the Lord's strength and shelter on that day.

_____

_____

_____

_____

_____

_____

_____

_____

_____

_____

_____

_____

18

GETTING PAST THE INNER PRESSURE TO BE SOMEONE YOU'RE NOT

I will praise thee; for I am fearfully and wonderfully made: marvellous are thy works; and that my soul knoweth right well.

PSALM 139:14

On Wednesday nights at church, I teach third- and fourth-grade kids about the Bible. This is my sweet spot, because on the inside I have the energetic and imaginative soul of a grade schooler. I can tell them Bible stories in ways that appeal to them, because God wonderfully made me with a kid-size imagination that I never outgrew. In this setting, I never feel like I have to pretend to be who I imagine a "mature" adult would be. I can be myself.

At work it's a different story. Every time I walk by the other high school teachers, I always have a strange, knee-jerk reaction. My immediate feeling is that the other teachers are all smarter than I am, better with students, more loving, kinder, experts in their fields. Where does this feeling come from? Not one of them has ever treated me as inferior. I've never heard an unkind word that would give me an impression of condescension.

That feeling of insecurity and inferiority followed me into the classroom, too. This came with a drive to pretend to be something that I wasn't. There was a foggy image in my mind of what a *good* teacher must look and act like, and I was reaching to grab hold of that, only to have it slip away.

Then one day I read something that said what my students need most is for me to be myself. This was a new idea to me. I soon realized I felt like everyone else is better than I am. One teacher seemed more intelligent—maybe I should be more like him. Another teacher wore more professional, classy clothes—maybe I should dress more like her. Another teacher seemed warmer and gentler toward students—maybe I should act more like him. Yet another teacher seemed more creative and fun in the classroom—maybe I should teach like him. I realized my enemy was whispering lies in my ear. The voice in my head was crippling me with an unrelenting sense of unworthiness.

But Psalm 139 says that I am wonderfully made, and I think that would include uniquely made. Other teachers don't think the way I do, because they don't have the same perspective, personality, life experiences, or spiritual gifts all mixed together. Other teachers don't teach the way I do, because they have been wonderfully made in different ways by God.

Now when I start to feel this way at school, I go to that verse and read that I am wonderfully made. ME. I have been designed by God in a marvelous way. You see where the psalmist says his soul knows this? My soul did not. My soul thought I was horribly and pathetically made. What an encouraging yet uncomfortable new truth to take into the classroom, into my church, and into my home with me: I am wonderfully made by a brilliant Creator, and to be myself in all settings is to honor how I was created to be. It feels strange to do this, though, which means I've had way too much practice pretending to be something I'm not rather than just being myself.

One day at school, I had my advanced Spanish students listen to a podcast set in Ecuador that really moved me. Before I embraced my true self, as created wonderfully by God, I would have played the podcast and then said, "Pretty cool, huh?" and moved on. But this time I allowed them to see my pure excitement. Childlike enthusiasm is who I am, but I've hidden it for so long in my attempts to be like the other teachers. In response, my students sat up and mirrored my enthusiasm. They received who I was, even though it felt weird to me, and it affected them in a positive way.

I think God wants us to be who he made us to be, and the people around us *need* us to bring the created elements of who we are in full authenticity all of the time. It just takes self-acceptance and practice.

JOURNAL: Describe a setting in which you keep feeling inferior and like you need to act a certain way around people. Now describe what it would look like for you to be completely yourself in that setting.

_____

_____

_____

_____

_____

_____

_____

_____

_____

_____

_____

_____

_____

19

SAY NO TO HOPELESS PESSIMISM

> *And we know that all things work together for good to them that love God, to them who are the called according to his purpose.*
>
> **ROMANS 8:28**

During the last two holiday seasons I came down with a virus, which turned into a lingering cough that lasted for five weeks. This past year I was totally healthy, not even the sniffles. Then came January, and I braced for the inevitable. Working at a school, you can almost see the germs crawling on every surface. I made sure my weekly lesson plans were ready for a substitute teacher, but then Friday would come and I'd still be healthy. Thank the Lord! Then came a week when I was launching the first all-church women's event for our women's ministry. It also coincided with the week we were studying illness vocabulary and verbs.

To vomit. To sneeze. To cough.

This had to be the week I was going to come down with the flu and be in bed for the first women's event and during the week when I was teaching my students about illness. I don't believe in the word *jinxed*, but it felt inevitable. How did this feeling of impending bad luck fit in with my belief in God? I reasoned that God surely couldn't blame me for my Eeyore pessimism. People get sick during the winter. I have to admit I believed God wouldn't be good to me when I wanted him to keep me healthy and energetic for the event I needed to lead.

Paul says to the believers in Rome (who are experiencing hard times) that when we love God, he is working everything for our good and for his purpose. I needed to let go of my idea of what was good. What if I were to get sick and miss the first event? Maybe God's purpose would be to allow my leadership team to shine and to humble me. That could be a good outcome that would glorify him. So, I worshipped the Lord and prayed, "Whatever you think is good for me and the women in my church, Lord, may that happen."

I did not get sick and felt great for the women's event; it was a rich night of worship and fellowship at our church. I also made it through "illness week" in my Spanish class with nary a sneeze. Both of those outcomes were good, but other, unpleasant outcomes might have been just as good. As I was leaving for home that Friday, I overheard the school secretary say many students were starting to get sick. For just a minute I panicked, but then I quickly turned my thoughts to the goodness of God. He cares about me, and even potential hard experience has his magnificent potential for good in it. I relaxed and put my trust in him.

JOURNAL: What horrible future possibility are you worrying yourself sick about? Make a list of all of the ways God has been good to you in the past, even in hard times, and allow that act of worship to rest your mind from worry.

A fool's wrath is presently known: but a prudent man covereth shame.

PROVERBS 12:16

20

OVERLOOKING A PROVOCATION

We used to live outside of the city limits, which we loved. The neighborhood was quiet, and the view from our back patio was a long line of snow-covered Rocky Mountains ending in a clear view of Glacier National Park. Every morning I would enjoy watching the sun poke its head over the mountain peaks, and in the winter, we would watch the spectacular alpine glow on the snowy ridge of mountains. Geese would fly overhead, and deer would walk through the yard. Our property was both majestic and serene.

But often our serene setting was disrupted by a boy in our neighborhood who kept busy with his noisy toys. In the summer, he drove his four-wheeler around his backyard for hours. When he got older, the four-wheeler turned into a motorbike. Around and around he would ride, motor roaring. In the middle of beautiful Montana summer days, we would have to close our back door to keep out the clouds of dust and the sound of the motorbike. In the winter, the motorbike was exchanged for a snowmobile or the four-wheeler pulling a sled with friends flying behind.

We never said anything, only sighed to each other. We didn't even talk about approaching the family about this. Matt and I both privately chose to swallow our annoyance. That's not so hard to do once, but it's extremely hard to do day after day after day, when the behavior of a neighbor's kid rubs against you like sandpaper. Every single time he annoyed me, I thought to myself, "I should just march over to his house, knock on the door, and express my frustration to his parents." But the Lord quietly stopped me every time. I felt the whisper to be patient—just be patient—and overlook it.

In the book of Proverbs, King Solomon advises the young men that a wise man covers over the shame or disgrace of someone else, like laying a coat over it so that no one can see. The other option is to make a big deal out of something, to get angry and speak out and call attention to the offending party. But to cover over an offense is to give the other person a taste of who Jesus is. I suppose Matt and I never said anything to the neighbors about their son's annoying behavior because we're so conscious of how much Jesus forgives and overlooks in us. We were friendly and simply covered up the offenses as if they had never happened.

The family moved away a number of years ago, and we were not sad. I see the dad sometimes, and we're friendly. He asks how our kids are doing; I ask how his son is doing. Matt and I don't seem to be the worse for wear. And if we grew in wisdom while we overlooked the noise and dust, then maybe we can consider the experience as being in our favor.

JOURNAL: Who has provoked you to anger lately—either in a small, annoying way or in a more significant, hurtful way? What have they done? Describe what a wise response on your part would be in covering over this offense.

21

OVERCOMING THE CONSTANT RUB OF LITTLE THINGS GONE WRONG

> *Rejoice in the Lord always:*
> *and again I say, Rejoice.*
>
> PHILIPPIANS 4:4

At 3:20 a.m., every smoke alarm in the house went off and we bolted out of bed. Matt scrambled for a ladder to turn off the alarms, while I made a quick pass through the house to see if there was any smoke or fire. It was what is called a rude awakening. *Rude* is a great word to describe all of the other small but annoying things that wear against us all throughout our days, like an itchy sweater.

The other day I was going about my morning and got all of the tasks on my list done. I had a leisurely time with the Lord, reading my Bible and praying. Then I emptied the dishwasher, made the bed, and graded some papers. I got in the shower, leaving myself plenty of time to get to school early and set up my classroom. As I was rinsing the conditioner out of my hair, the thought struck me that it was a Tuesday—a special schedule day at our school. My class started at 10:21, instead of 10:36 like I was planning for. I rushed through getting dressed, called the school, and ran into class, breathless and frazzled, one minute after the bell rang. It was a rude beginning to my school day.

If we were to keep a running tally of every time some little thing went wrong, whether it was our own fault or something out of our control, I would guess we would be able to list many discouraging experiences in a day. How should we handle this assault of mishaps within our spirits? Paul says to rejoice in the Lord always, and that's the command I pull up when something goes south in my day.

My gut reaction is to be angry or frustrated, but I try to move quickly to the purposeful act of looking to the Lord and finding my joy in him. I often say, "Lord, you are good," even when the moment doesn't feel good. I try to switch toward thanking him instead of griping and groaning. It's hard work. The tally of bad things that can happen in a day is high, and I don't want to live in discontent and complaining. I would rather do the mental labor to rejoice in the Lord *always*.

The morning after our smoke alarm fiasco, Matt climbed up the ladder to the living room ceiling to reattach the alarm, but it wouldn't thread. He must have tried a dozen times until it finally worked. It was just another one of those small but frustrating moments in life when it's easy to think that everything is always so hard. But we need to practice moving our thinking to rejoicing in the Lord in each of these difficult moments.

JOURNAL: List a few of the small rubs of frustration that have happened to you over the last few days. What was your immediate response to them? Describe what it could have looked like to rejoice in one of those little trials.

22

OVERCOMING HURT FEELINGS

> *Now the serpent was more subtil than any beast of the field which the LORD God had made. And he said unto the woman, Yea, hath God said, Ye shall not eat of every tree of the garden?*
>
> **GENESIS 3:1**

I got my feelings hurt by someone I knew. Emotionally, I was on the ground and could not stand up, like when someone sneaks up on you and pokes your knees and you collapse. For a week I couldn't sleep, my stomach was upset, and I had a hard time concentrating at work.

The act that hurt my feelings was trivial. When I told Matt, it sounded like a middle school complaint. But the feeling of hurt was deep, even though there was no evil intention on the part of the offender. I will admit that my obsessive personality doesn't sit well in these situations. I mentally drive whatever it is that happened into the ground—a toxic replay of what happened and how I felt about it, with all of the shards of injustice repeatedly piercing my mind. Her. Me. Injustice. Her. Me. Injustice. Her. Me. Injustice.

During this time, I was reading *The Soul of Shame* by Curt Thompson. He took me to the story of Adam and Eve in the Bible, in which "Mr. Crafty," a.k.a. Satan, does this subtle work of getting Eve to start talking with him *about* God instead of her talking *to* God. I realized I was doing the same thing. I was mentally bringing in Scripture, because I wanted to handle my feelings in a God-honoring way. But I was also independently thinking about how to handle the situation, using my very good imagination to create selfish responses. It was ugly.

After one week of making myself ill, I finally looked to God and asked how he wanted me to handle it. G. K. Chesterton says in *Orthodoxy*, it's like opening the door of a third-class carriage going "round and round the Inner Circle" and "getting out at Gower Street." Talking to God took me out of the vicious cycle of my own thinking and allowed me to hear truth from him. God immediately spoke to my heart, saying that I needed to talk to this dear person in my life, instead of emotionally punishing her with my cool withdrawal.

That prospect made me want to throw up, and it took me a full half hour to work up the courage to call her. Once she answered the phone, I immediately started bawling (very middle school), and we had a good talk. It wasn't a perfect fix, but we cleared the air and took steps to repair our relationship.

God is good. But the crafty serpent wanted to pull my eyes and heart away from God, just as he did with Eve in the garden. It was a cycle that only added more pain. It would have destroyed me if I had never opened the door of that cheap carriage and stepped out. I learned we must talk directly to God. We must look up and ask him what to do, instead of trying to figure it out in our own minds.

JOURNAL: Has anyone hurt your feelings? What has been happening in your mind since that hurt? Write a prayer of looking to God and asking him to help you get out of a bad cycle of thinking.

23

HANDING OFF YOUR WORRY TO SOMEONE WHO CARES

> *Casting all your care upon him;*
> *for he careth for you.*
>
> **1 PETER 5:7**

The phone call came on a February night. I sat at the kitchen barstool while my mom and brother told me my dad had died. The men had been out snowmobiling in Wyoming, and Dad fell over and died nearly instantly of a probable heart attack. My brother performed CPR for an hour in an attempt to resuscitate him. It was one of the most painful nights of my life.

But nothing prepared me for the deeper, more ongoing pain I would experience over the coming months for my now-widowed mother. Every phone call included tears.

Every conversation included the hard realities of a woman trying to figure out how to do all of the things regarding the home and finances instead of just half the things. With every visit I tried to grieve with my mom and also bring some laughter and lightheartedness.

The hardest part was living 12 hours away in northern Montana, while my mom lives in central Wyoming. I couldn't have her over for a cup of tea after a hard day, stop in to give her a hug and see how she was doing, or even just help around the house. Saying goodbye to my dad unexpectedly was a great sorrow, but the daily pain of a grieving widow was crushing my heart. A daughter should be able to do something, but this was something my mom had to go through alone.

One December after my dad had passed, I was doing Christmassy things, and I thought of my mom doing the holiday season by herself, with no one in the house to appreciate her beautiful decorations and Christmas tree. No one with whom to watch Christmas movies. No one for whom to bake cookies. I can't describe the weight of grief I felt for her that day. I sat down on the floor in the living room and cried while I prayed for her. It was a guttural cry, begging God somehow to help my mom find some joy in the season. I prayed all afternoon that he would take care of her and help her be happy.

The next day I called my mom. She told me her friends had invited her out to lunch, and they had toured a huge collection of nativity scenes at a local church. She described in detail to me all of the different and unique nativity scenes they had seen. Her voice was happy, full of life, and overflowing with joy.

Just the day before, I had sobbed on the living room floor, begging God to take care of my mom's heart, but he was already on it. In fact, he was in the middle of answering my prayer. I was going through Kleenex, and she was walking around with a friend enjoying Christmas. Amazing. I cast my anxiety for my mom on the Lord, and he showed me how much he cared for her. And it wasn't a necessity. A woman doesn't *need* to have fun at Christmas, but the Lord was so kind. He was so generous to see my pain in the season and answer my prayer in a personal way. God really cares about us.

JOURNAL: What anxieties are you carrying for someone in your life? What is it you wish God would do for this person? Write an honest prayer, telling him what's weighing on you and asking him to show his kindness.

God resisteth the proud, but
giveth grace unto the humble.

JAMES 4:6

24

ENDURING A SEASON OF HUMILIATION

I found out about my current job opening at around 8 a.m. and had signed the contract by noon. The job of high school Spanish teacher was mine, and I was thrilled. Oh, and school started in two weeks.

Arrangements were made for me to meet the previous teacher so that she could explain what she had done and show me the supplies. However, the previous teacher was actually a gymnastics coach who had lived in Spain for a while and could speak fluent Spanish. When I walked into the room, there wasn't much to show me. No lesson plans. No supplies. When I asked her what she had been teaching, I could write everything she said on one side of an index card.

I had received my teaching credential 20 years earlier. Before this job, I only had one year of teaching experience with third graders. Adding to all of this, I only minored in Spanish. I loved the language, but I hadn't used it for two decades. In a sense, I was going back to school myself to relearn the language. I knew how to teach, but I had never taught Spanish, so I had to refresh my own familiarity with vocabulary and grammar while trying to figure out the best way to teach the language. I created everything from scratch, making or buying what I needed.

Since I was in a new school, I didn't know the teachers, the students, or the culture of the school. I didn't know where to park or how to open the old windows. Even the computer programs the teachers used were new to me. Then there was my classroom. It was located in a building that used to be a nursing home, in a room that should have hosted one elderly person and a dresser. The heat of a cramped space, plus the nerves from teaching 23 students in such a small space, was stressful. That first year I'd find myself lecturing with my arms by my side so that my students couldn't see me sweat.

This was the most humiliating year of my life. At every turn, I felt inept and green and cowardly. Failure seemed imminent every day. Just when I thought I finally had my feet beneath me, a new challenge would appear the following day.

But it was during this year that I said goodbye to pride and experienced God's grace in ways I never had before. There, in the land of the novice teacher, I became desperately dependent on the Lord and grew deep roots in him because of my constant neediness. I was a new teacher with no lesson plans, and he filled my mind with ideas. I felt new and alone, but he felt close and helpful. I called out to him in my inadequacy, and he kept assuring me that he loved my humility and would compensate for my weakness.

Most of my prayers during that time were simple: "Jesus, help me." The prayers of an exhausted, humbled woman who desperately needed strength to carry on despite feelings of insecurity and inadequacy (not to mention the sweat) were blunt. I didn't have the energy to be eloquent. "Help," I said. I knew God was right there with me, and I knew help would come. It was the most spiritually rich year I've ever experienced. I would never want to go through that again, but I wouldn't trade it for anything.

JOURNAL: What is the most humiliating thing you've experienced lately? How has that experience positively affected your relationship with God?

25

LET TIRING CHORES
LEAD TO STRONG ARMS

She girdeth her loins with strength,
and strengtheneth her arms.

PROVERBS 31:17

The storm came in during the night, and Matt had to leave early for work. I cheerfully put on snow boots, hat, and gloves and grabbed a shovel. We have a snowblower, but I like the workout of scooping snow and hefting it onto the growing bank. It felt good to work hard, and it made my cheeks pink with the fresh, cold air.

That afternoon I also spent time in our crawl space, bent in half and carrying boxes of Christmas decorations back to where they belonged. (Matt is six feet two, so we have an agreement that the short wife will do the crawl space work.) I also did a load of laundry and emptied the dishwasher. After that I went to three different stores. I emptied the carts full of bags into the trunk and then went home and carried all of the groceries into the house and put everything away. It was a very physical day.

In Proverbs 31 we read the description of a noble wife, and I find it interesting that she is a woman who puts her back into her work, does the heavy lifting and the sweating, and lets her muscles rip. Certainly, there is work I'm not strong enough to do, and I ask Matt to help me with those tasks. There are things I can't reach and boxes I can't lift. But the farther I go along, the more I realize I was created to do the kind of work that builds muscle. I can manage the crawl space, shovel snow, and bring in groceries, all in the same day. This is who God made me to be.

Hard work can be a drudgery. It can feel like all of this labor is shoved at us, and we're trapped beneath it—nothing but work from sunup to sundown. Or hard work can be a joy and a discovery that this is what we were made for. The muscles God crafted within our bodies are of glorious design and are the tools given to us to love our families well. Proverbs 31 talks about a wife of noble character, and I believe she's a woman whose arms are strong.

I love shoveling snow. I get hot with sweat and have to take off my gloves and unzip my coat. As I push snow, I think about how happy Matt will be that it won't melt and turn into ice on the driveway. This is noble work.

JOURNAL: How do you feel about using your muscles to serve your family? Drudgery or honor? Describe a time when you developed strong arms in doing challenging housework.

26

DON'T CHOOSE STRESS WHEN YOU DON'T HAVE TO

> *Take therefore no thought for the morrow: for the morrow shall take thought for the things of itself. Sufficient unto the day is the evil thereof.*
>
> MATTHEW 6:34

I call my monthly calendar my horizontal calendar. Recently, the activities listed throughout the week were causing me to hyperventilate. Tuesday appeared impossible. Wednesday impossible. February impossible. This whole year looks to be impossible. Probably my entire life is impossible. Where's a brown paper bag for me to breath into?

On my way to work I reprimanded myself about stressing over my commitments, fretting that I was going to make myself sick and drive Matt nuts. An image came into my mind of someone running a sprint versus a marathon. The weight of my future schedule was causing me to live in an unsustainable, high-energy mode, instead of chugging along at a challenging but doable pace. So, there in the car, on my way to work, I decided to go vertical.

A vertical calendar means to view the day from sunup to sundown—from morning to night with a hard stop at bedtime. Instead of looking forward to the future, vertical means only looking at today. It's a simple biblical concept from Jesus's own lips. Doesn't the vertical day, from morning to night, have enough trouble of its own? Jesus is reasonable.

As I pulled off of the highway and onto the street heading to school, I thought about my day and how to shift my schedule around so that I didn't feel the need to reach for a paper bag. The personal questions change when you go vertical. Instead of saying, "How am I going to make it through this next week?" you ask, "Can I live vibrantly until lunch?"

I don't want to be a stressed-out lady, and Jesus doesn't want me to live that way either. I prayed, "Lord, I want to live. I don't want to just survive and go from one insane day to the next. I want to work hard on this day but also enjoy the people who cross my path and be able to give a relaxed smile to everyone I meet."

I don't regret changing my point of view from horizontal to vertical that morning. I don't regret calming down and only tackling the seven work hours in front of me. I don't regret my ability to walk into school and greet the school secretary with an authentic and cheerful "Good morning!" The question is, can I continue to live life with my focus on vertical living? I think I can.

JOURNAL: What are you worrying about in the days stretching ahead of you on the calendar? How would your feelings about persevering change if you were just to focus on this one day, from sunup to sundown?

27

WHEN YOUR PEOPLE DRIVE YOU TO THE EDGE OF YOUR TEMPER

> *Wherefore, my beloved brethren, let every man be swift to hear, slow to speak, slow to wrath.*
>
> **JAMES 1:19**

I had to fight back tears after my freshmen Spanish class, because my students were making me nuts. I had planned an especially challenging week for the class for mastering some new information. There was no time for slacking. It was going to be a busy day, so I asked them to work for 20 minutes without talking to each other.

But do you think they could do that?

One student asked if he could get something out of his locker. A minute later, I saw him walk back in while unwrapping a sandwich and carrying two other food items. When I made him go put it all back in his locker, he acted like I was crazy. Another student foraged around in his backpack while I was giving the instructions. Four students in succession asked if they could go to the bathroom, which is code for "This is boring. Let's get outta here."

I spent the 20-minute study session telling students to "turn around," "quit talking," "get to work," and "face the front, please." I was on my last nerve, so I did what any teacher who was totally unprepared for such a display of disrespect would do on a Monday morning: I lectured them. Because everyone knows teens *love* a good lecture that calls out their bad behavior.

"I'm disappointed in this class. You all need to grow in self-control. This week is going to be hard, and you've wasted time," I said sternly while standing in front of the class.

I will admit I was in tears after class. Later that day, I thought of wiser actions I could have taken instead of spewing words of disappointment. I could have removed a few of the disruptive students from class. I could have rode out the storm of bad behavior and then, after calming down, administered consequences the next day. But instead I felt like I lost control and failed. I knew more professional ways to handle the situation, but they disappeared from mind when I most needed them. It seems like all good rational ideas come usually right after you've blown it, right? I talked to Matt on the phone later in the afternoon. He naively asked how my day had gone, and I told him my story. But then I said, "Well, God's mercies are new every day, and tomorrow I'll try this thing again."

Anger isn't bad. My misbehaving students deserved my anger, but I let it flare up instead of thinking about how to handle it in a way that was calm and would produce better behavior. Nobody benefits from a fast flare of anger instead of a well-thought-out, slow response. Tomorrow I'll pray my way into class more fervently and look for ways to be patient and loving with students who are working toward maturity the same way I am. Lord willing, I'll show them how it's done by exercising the kind of self-control I wish they had exercised.

JOURNAL: How do you usually handle your anger? Write out a scenario regarding something that always makes you angry and what it would look like to be self-controlled and slower to anger.

*Thy word is a lamp unto my feet,
and a light unto my path.*

PSALM 119:105

28

WHEN YOU'RE DERAILED BY YOUR EMOTIONS

Two of my high school students came to my classroom at the beginning of lunch and asked if they could eat inside with me. This was unusual, but I was happy to let them hang out. While I sat working at my desk, I could easily hear their conversation; they weren't trying to hide it. It wasn't long before I could tell they were very upset about something that happened during a sports practice. This dispute had been causing anguish in their minds and hearts since the evening before, and their conversation was emotionally charged. It seemed they were trying to figure out how to respond to the challenge they were experiencing.

I was having the same kind of experience in my personal life, so their conversation resonated. Someone had hurt me, and I felt completely derailed. I was having a hard time sleeping and couldn't figure out how to respond. It was strange to hear my own secret torment of emotions being echoed by these students. I almost wanted to thank them for saying out loud what I was feeling, even though the circumstances were completely different.

The students didn't know that I had spent almost two hours that morning fiercely holding on to Biblical truths by my fingernails. My emotions were trying to bully me into reacting poorly to this person who had hurt me, but I had too much of the Bible in my mind for the emotions to gain the higher ground. However, being obedient to all of that truth in the heat of emotions felt like trying to swim with all of my clothes on.

It occurred to me that this was Navy SEAL-level training for the soul. I've always been intrigued by the intensity of their training and their determination never to quit. They say their nation expects them to be stronger than their enemies, and they simply will never give up.

I think we have to be stronger than the enemy that our emotions sometimes are. Feelings war against us. They try to get us to respond to the people in our lives via self-pity, annoyance, passive-aggressiveness, sarcasm, silent treatments, or flashes of anger. But when we follow Jesus, we are not permitted to act however we want. We're called to his kingdom's standard, and it is a Navy SEAL kind of hard.

JOURNAL: What strong emotion derailed you most recently? How did you respond? In what ways did you search out and obey the instructions in Scripture that shone light on how you should act in that situation?

_____

_____

_____

_____

_____

_____

_____

_____

_____

_____

_____

_____

_____

_____

_____

_____

_____

29

USING DELAYS TO GROW
IN PATIENCE

> *But the fruit of the Spirit is love, joy,
> peace, longsuffering, gentleness,
> goodness, faith, meekness, temperance:
> against such there is no law.*
>
> GALATIANS 5:22-23

We moved in with Matt's mom and aunt a few years ago to help out around the place. I wanted to create a sitting area in our bedroom where we could have some private time together, but we don't have the kind of income that supports splurges on furniture.

Finally, the Lord gave me an opportunity. Chairs were on sale at Costco for $50 off, but the sale ended the next day. I texted Matt a picture, and he said, "Do it." (Bless him!) I pushed a flat cart to the front of the store, loaded with our two new chairs.

The store was insane. I picked the absolute worst day to make this huge purchase. The Super Bowl was the next day. I think it's fair to say the entire town of Kalispell was there that afternoon. But I didn't let the long lines deter my purchases and waited patiently. When it was my time to pay, the cashier said, "That will be $350."

"What?" I said. "They were each supposed to be $50 off. It should be $300."

That's when it began: me holding up the line on the day before the Super Bowl. I could imagine all of the people wanting to hurry up, buy their food, and get home, which made me anxious. My face turned red, and I started saying, "Sorry, sorry, sorry." But I couldn't take a $50 hit just to free up the line. The cashier called for a supervisor, but no one came. She hollered out to a manager to help. He had to run all the way to the back of the store to get the price sign for the chairs. Then he came back, he got another supervisor, and they deleted the previous sale and started over. This time the discount for both chairs went through, and the dam of humanity my debacle had created was broken loose.

It felt like this took an hour.

I have been on that waiting side of things before, when the person in front of me has forgotten their money or their item was rung up at the wrong price. It's quite a test of faith in those situations. We can choose either to be complete jerks and dump more discomfort on the person holding up the line or to slow our breathing and ask God to help us exercise a godly generosity of patience and grace.

Experiences of waiting give us an opportunity to show others the beauty and goodness of Jesus. But it's hard. Let's admit it's really hard and takes a fierce amount of self-control. What a gift, though. I'm so thankful for the kind folks in line behind me at Costco.

JOURNAL: Write an honest description of how you usually respond when you are forced into a position of waiting. Now write a list of good thought habits you could develop in those moments, and practice saying them out loud a few times.

_____

_____

_____

_____

_____

_____

_____

_____

_____

_____

_____

_____

_____

_____

_____

_____

_____

30

PUTTING DOWN YOUR OWN TO-DO LIST TO SERVE WHEN NEEDED

For whosoever will save his life shall lose it: and whosoever will lose his life for my sake shall find it.

MATTHEW 16:25

My day was full. I spent my morning personal time, normally reserved for Bible reading and prayer, thinking of how I would teach school that day. After a full day at school, I would hit the ground running when I got home from work. I needed to get my thoughts together for leading a two-hour women's ministry planning meeting that night, and I also had to make tacos for the meeting. I had a lot of work ahead of me.

The day before, I had found out a dear friend was having a big surgery in a few days. It came up really fast for her, and her family had moved into a new house just three days prior. I prayed for her. Then I faced the reality that if I were a true friend in Christ, I would do more than just pray. This was a painful moment. My day was already full of things I had to do, but my friend needed help right now. So, I looked to God and said, "If I help her, will you help me?" I knew from past experience, without even asking this, that if I would lay down my own life to serve someone, God would use his power to make up the difference so that I could fulfill my own obligations.

I texted my friend, "How can I help you today? My afternoon is open." The response was fast. Her blood iron was low, and she could barely function. She was hoping to go in for a blood transfusion in the afternoon. She asked if I could stop by to do some laundry and organize her kitchen and pantry.

"Did you just ask me to do my two favorite things in the whole world?" I texted back.

I told her I would be over at 2 p.m., and I planned to help for a few hours. I didn't know how in the world I was going to get ready for my meeting and help her, but I was trusting that God was going to help me extend myself in that way. I had tested him in this kind of situation so many times that I knew he was somehow going to make the hours a little bit longer for me.

This was an opportunity to love my friend with laundry detergent and my mad organizational skills. It was going to cost me something, but this was the good life Jesus modeled for us. Obedience in service would help my friend, but it also would benefit my own soul.

JOURNAL: When is the last time you inconvenienced yourself to help someone in need? What did it cost you? How did you see God provide what you needed for your own life?

_____

_____

_____

_____

_____

_____

_____

_____

_____

_____

_____

_____

_____

_____

_____

_____

_____

31

THE MOST PRODUCTIVE WOMEN KNOW HOW TO REST

> *And God blessed the seventh day and sanctified it: because that in it he had rested from all his work which God created and made.*
>
> **GENESIS 2:3**

I was sitting at my desk thinking about writing a devotion on the subject of rest when I immediately felt sleepy. (Impending work will do that to you.) It was a dark afternoon, and the rain was coming down hard against my office window. Instead of turning to open my laptop, I went to the bedroom, crawled under a cozy quilt, and took a little snooze. One thing I've learned is how to rest my mind and body so that I am energized to continue the day's work that lies in front of me.

By now you've read about my experiences as a teacher. I always carry around Spanish lesson plans and concern for students in my mind. I'm also a writer, so a lot of my time is spent reading, learning, and thinking about what value I could present to my readers. Add into the mix my position as director of the women's ministry at church, and my brain is also filled with planning events and thinking about connecting with women. Oh, and I teach children the Bible on Wednesday nights, which is kind of like preparing a 25-minute sermon every week, but for a wiggly audience. It requires a lot of creative thinking. I bet you want to nap just reading about all of my responsibilities.

Women do complex work, because God has made us in an incredible, magnificent way. We can manage a wide variety of work—caring for many people, thinking through many tasks—all at the same time. However, our brains get tired and need rest, and we must not feel guilty about that. Consider the complex design of our brains and how much better they function when they can be quieted on a regular basis.

We need moments in every day when we purposefully stop accomplishing and allow ourselves to sit in a chair to look out of the window, sit on the front step, or climb under a blanket for a power nap. This is not laziness; it's purposeful care for the body and mind God has given us.

When we rest, our renewed mental and physical energy is a gift to our families. Well-rested women are able to serve and love people in a sustainable way.

JOURNAL: List all of your main responsibilities. Now write ways you can rest from these in small moments during the day and then one day a week. Describe how this rest will improve how you carry out your responsibilities.

*For we are his workmanship,
created in Christ Jesus unto good works,
which God hath before ordained that
we should walk in them.*

EPHESIANS 2:10

32

MAINTAINING PURPOSE IN LIFE AS YOU GET OLDER

I recently bought the best multivitamin recommended for women over 50. It was a sobering moment. "How did I get to this stage of life?" I mumbled to myself as I reached for my readers in my purse. Wasn't it just yesterday that I had hugged my firstborn daughter, who was now 30 weeks pregnant? Recently, her round belly reached me before she did, and when I gave her a hug, the little guy kicked me! It was wonderful, but at the same time it left me feeling overwhelmed. In a very short time, I was going to become a grandma. Aren't grandmas old? I was talking to my mom right after I officially became women's ministry director for our church. I was telling her all about how I felt inadequate for the position and not wise enough.

"Honey," she said. "I'm sorry to tell you this, but you're old enough to have what it takes to fill this position."

I mean, really.

She was right, of course. I've been married almost 29 years and raised two kids. I've worked several jobs and learned how to be a homemaker. I've walked through misunderstandings in marriage, parenting struggles, financial strains, friendship fractures, character fails, and various levels of grief. I've also learned how to pray, how to study the Bible, how to know God, and how to depend on the Lord in the big and little circumstances of life.

Now here I am in my fifties. My kids are grown. I have a lot of free time, so I'm using my days to say *yes* to the Lord. Yes, I'll teach kids the Bible on Wednesday nights. Yes, I'll use my writing to help people understand the Bible. Yes, I'll invest in the lives of the women of my church. Yes, I'll help out my mother-in-law and her sister.

I could be playing. I think a lot of women see the empty-nest years as the time when they finally get to live for themselves. I don't mind a little indulgence now that the kids are grown, especially the luxury of losing myself in a good book, but I'm too aware of the needs of this world to overindulge myself all of the time. How can I live my life playing when people are hurting and have deep needs?

I could be moping. I know so many women who grieve as if their lives have ended when the kids leave the nest. But I've been following Jesus, and he is my life. I love my precious kids, but when they left home, my life was still centered on the Lord. Following him and doing the good work he puts in front of me every day doesn't leave time for moping.

I could be wandering around lost. However, it seems to me that would show a great lack of awareness about how much value I have to offer other people. God has been shaping my life to be of encouragement to others. How could I be lost? God has plenty of good work for me to do to fill up my days.

So, I'll take a multivitamin made for women in their fifties and live the coming decade with full energy. My life has purpose, because God has designed my days, and that design didn't stop when my birthday brought me into a new season of life.

JOURNAL: In what ways does God give your life meaning? How will that meaning and purpose continue as you get older?

_____

_____

_____

_____

_____

_____

_____

_____

33

DON'T BE AFRAID TO ASK GOD FOR HELP

> *If any of you lack wisdom, let him ask of God, that giveth to all men liberally, and upbraideth not; and it shall be given him.*
>
> JAMES 1:5

I was the kid who sat in the front row in every class, notebook open, an eager expression on my face, ready to learn. That is, until sixth-grade math. That math teacher was mean and unpredictable. If he called on you and you answered wrong, he made you look and feel like a fool in front of everybody. If you asked him for help, he treated you like you were an idiot. Sometimes he would just make fun of students for no good reason. In that class I learned to stay quiet as an act of self-preservation.

Now I'm the teacher, and I can feel the weight of my influence in how I respond to students when they ask for help. Every Friday we have a Spanish test, and I have schooled myself in proper body language to let students know I'm there to help them. When students raise their hands, I look them in the eyes, smile, and walk quickly to help. After I've answered the question, I send another warm smile that I hope says, "Thank you for asking."

Often while my students are taking a test, I'll announce that I love answering questions, so they shouldn't be shy to ask for help. I also try to reward them by being shockingly generous. It's important to me that they associate raising their hands with getting a generous reward for taking the risk. Many times, I give helpful hints, or I just say, "Yes, you're right on that."

We all need a lot of help in this life, so when it comes to our relationship with God, we need to know whom we're dealing with. Is God like my sixth-grade math teacher, looking for any excuse to humiliate me and make me feel stupid? Or is God like a generous teacher who has a warm heart toward students and stands ready to help when asked? Should I cower quietly in a self-protective mode or boldly raise my voice in prayer and ask for anything that I need from God, expecting to get a joyful and good-willed response?

I believe I found the answer in the verse from the book of James quoted at the beginning of this chapter. I fell in love with the phrase "upbraideth not." If you go to God and ask him for wisdom about something, he will not rail, chide, or taunt you. He is nothing like my sixth-grade math teacher. Instead, God gives wisdom to those who ask, and he gives it liberally. In the original Greek, the word in that verse means he gives simply and sincerely, led solely by his desire to bless.

If we know God is this warm and well-intentioned toward us, then we are fools if we do not learn to raise our hands and ask for wisdom constantly.

JOURNAL: How have you always imagined God would respond if you were to ask him for wisdom? How does James 1:5 change how you'll pray in the future?

34

DO YOU FEEL YOU'RE NOT GOOD ENOUGH TO SERVE GOD?

Unto me, who am less than the least of all saints, is this grace given, that I should preach among the Gentiles the unsearchable riches of Christ.

EPHESIANS 3:8

"I just found the most amazing verse," I told my preacher husband.

"Oh, and what is that?" he asked.

"Paul says he was less than the least of all God's people," I told him. "But God still chose him to tell people about Jesus. Paul, the person we look up to as one of the great apostles of Christ, says he was less than the least! Isn't that wonderful?"

Matt and I share similar callings that present themselves in different ways of service. Matt is a Bible study teacher on Tuesday nights and a preacher on the weekend. He also teaches a few weeks every year at a Bible college near Glacier National Park that our church founded a few years ago. I teach the Bible to kids on Wednesday nights, and I write devotional blog posts and books to help people know God.

We also have in common something I call "exposure sickness." It's a miserable, gnawing feeling of great unworthiness that we both experience after we've been brave enough to stand up and teach people about Jesus. It's all of the insecurity that rises up when we've been at a microphone and have opened ourselves up in order to teach the Bible from the heart.

Imagine our delight when I found Paul's words about being "less than the least of all God's people." When I shared the verse with him, Matt looked it up in the original Greek and discovered the word *elachistoteros*, which has the word "least" with the phrase "less than" tucked inside of it like creamy cookie filling.

Now when exposure sickness hits, and one of us finds ourselves mumbling our insecurities, we say to one another, "Elachistoteros."

We learn from Paul that inflating one another's self-esteem isn't the cure for exposure sickness. The cure is honesty. Who are we to be Bible teachers or writers or preachers? Matt and I both know how unworthy we are, and we feel it constantly. But the cure for this vulnerable awareness of weakness is admitting that it is only the grace of God that gives us a reason to take pen in hand or pick up a microphone. Matt and I quote Paul in saying we are less than the least, and we argue in bed at night about which one of us is really less than. Even so, we rejoice that, despite our condition, God has graced us with the joy of serving him with the gifts he has given us.

JOURNAL: What work do you feel God has graced you to do in service to his kingdom? Describe the feeling of unworthiness you battle when it comes to carrying out this work.

35

CONTROL THE URGE TO OWN ALL OF THE PRETTY THINGS

> *Lay not up for yourselves treasures upon earth, where moth and rust doth corrupt, and where thieves break through and steal.*
>
> MATTHEW 6:19

My daughter Jayme gave me a gift card to Target for my birthday, and I wanted some new towels. (Things moms buy for fun, eh?) On my list was also a plastic bin, for storing something at church. You know how this goes. I entered through the front doors and turned to stare at the Starbucks. It was 3:30 p.m., and I had a gift card in my wallet. But did I really need coffee? I talked myself out of it and kept walking.

Next I stopped at the shelving just past the Starbucks. Look at those cute baskets on display! Round ones and square ones, in soft earth tones—my favorite colors. Imagine how cute those would be in my linen closet. *I need those.* The craving to buy things was strong, a feeling of deep and insatiable hunger within me. *Emptiness!* I preached to myself. I knew accumulating pretty items would satisfy like a handful of cotton candy: a momentary pleasure.

I headed toward the towels by way of the Magnolia section.

Is there a woman strong enough to go to Target without perusing this section and dreaming of owning all of Joanna Gaines's creativity? I admired cute tiered shelving, beautiful table runners, black measuring cups, and a beautiful black dish. I finally made it to the towel section and found a set of white ones with a thin gray stripe at the bottom.

I am taking you through my Target route because I want to talk about our strong urge to own pretty things. Jesus says we shouldn't store up treasures on earth, because they just don't last. He must have known someday there would be a Target and a Joanna Gaines. It's really a question of satisfaction. Do I satisfy my heart about two millimeters deep for a half hour by filling my cart with the loveliness on the Target shelves, or do I hold out for a deeper satisfaction that comes from seeking the kind of treasure you can't scan and put on a charge card?

JOURNAL: What store or website draws your attention and makes you want to accumulate stuff for yourself? Describe a specific way that seeking God's kingdom treasure has satisfied you more deeply than anything you've ever bought for yourself.

Honour thy father and thy mother . . .

EXODUS 20:12

36

CARING FOR AGING PARENTS

My daughter, at age 19, was engaged to be married in May. My dad had passed away just four months before that, a few years before he was to turn 70. I was shocked to find those two things happening at the same time. I naively had imagined myself living a long life and then, near the end of it, caring for my aging parents. How was it possible that my dad was gone, my mom was a widow, and both of my children were still teenagers? We weren't even empty-nesters yet. Wasn't there supposed to be a huge gap of enjoying life after your kids are grown and long before your own parents need any help? My bubble of misconception had popped.

My mom was on her own, and I observed my brother and his wife helping her out. She was in great health, but she was still a woman left alone to manage the house, property, possessions, and finances. I watched my brother and his wife and kids lovingly drive five hours a few times a month to help her out. It was so beautiful, and I found myself longing to be that kind of person toward my mother-in-law and her sister, who are here in the town where we live.

When our son was still in high school, Matt and I started talking about caring for his mom and aunt and what that would look like for us. It's a sensitive subject, because people's dignity is at stake. We saw it was getting harder for the ladies to take care of their house and acre of property. We started to think, pray, and talk about this, because we had a strong desire to honor Matt's mom as she was getting older, as well as her sister, who had always been single.

One summer, after Matt and I paid an exorbitant amount of money to have someone mow their lawn, we had a serious conversation. We considered selling our house and building one that would work for us all to live in together, but in the end, we realized it was wise for us to move in with them and help out around the place.

It was a great decision. We were present to see the dishwasher smoking one day and were able to take care of getting it replaced immediately. We mow the lawn and take the garbage to the dump. We've also found a richness in being around to answer Jeopardy questions and solve Wheel of Fortune puzzles every evening. It's not always easy, though, for all of us. Three women with three very different personalities in a house can cause clashes. In all honesty, I sometimes long for my own home. But at the end of the day, it has been a joy to love Matt's mom and aunt in a real way. We want to be present for as long as they need us.

The easy thing would be not to help, not to give up anything, and not to bend our own lives and plans toward parents who need us. But God's design is for us to honor our fathers and mothers, to let their welfare carry a heavy weight in our minds and hearts. That call takes on a deeper significance as our parents get older.

JOURNAL: Describe someone you know who has set an example in caring for an aging parent. What have you admired about their decisions and actions?

37

ARE YOU FRUSTRATED BY A DEEP PASSION FOR WHICH YOU HAVE NO OUTLET?

> *. . . thou hast been faithful over a few things, I will make thee ruler over many things.*
>
> MATTHEW 25:21

For one year, God started communicating to me, in the privacy of my own heart, his desire that I run the women's ministry at my church. No one at the church or the women's ministry had said anything to me. The idea was brought to me totally from the Lord. My gut response was to say, "Eeeewww, no thanks." But he kept talking.

I wasn't willing to stiff-arm the Lord, but I was a hard sell. Even so, I continued to listen. Being a leader was not something I had ever desired. The responsibilities of being the director and planning activities made me break into hives. Still, he continued to speak to me. A woman I had met only once dropped off a book for me at church. Matt brought it home, and it was filled with the stories of the Calvary Chapel wives. Every single chapter ended by saying, "And now she's women's ministry director at her church." The Lord could not have been more obvious; as a pastor's wife I could take great leadership in guiding women in my church.

I talked to a friend in Texas, and she was going on about how her church was exploding in growth and how exciting it was for the members. I asked her if she could pinpoint the cause of that growth, and she said, "Oh, it's the women's ministry. It's so vibrant that women are coming, and then their husbands and children start to attend church with them."

I gulped.

I had demands for the Lord, respectfully. In my mind, I could only see women gathering for tea parties and craft nights, which weren't my cup of tea. (See what I did there?) One day, I told him I longed for spiritually rich activities that meet the deep needs of women. Just then, I happened upon a blog post that listed what women are really looking for in ministry in our day, and the list matched the list I had just whispered to the Lord.

"Lord, surely you're not serious about me doing this," I kept saying. But he was, and he continued to speak to me for an entire year. I couldn't turn around without hearing "women's ministry, women's ministry, women's ministry."

But when I finally agreed, another woman in our church was placed in the position.

For years—years, I tell you—I raised my hands in question to God. Why in the world did I receive this obvious call to a position and then have the door closed to me? Over the next several years, my ideas for women's ministry and my passion for the hearts of women grew, yet still the door was closed. So, I waited.

While I waited—often exasperated and confused—I grew on the inside. I learned about the hearts of women through a class I taught at church. I climbed the ladder of success in my writing life and learned to be satisfied in doing the smaller work God had put in front of me. My faith grew. My knowledge of God's word grew. I planned my daughter's wedding and learned I am capable of coordinating a big event. I started a small group for four single women, and I found deep satisfaction in this. Maybe this was the women's ministry God had designed for me after all?

Then, seven years after God originally approached me about filling the women's ministry director position, the door opened. The role became mine. The *yes* of seven years prior became a green light. I had no idea God needed this time to grow me into a woman ready to be a leader of women. It was a long wait. During that time, I learned to be faithful in small things. In the end, God saw my faithfulness and decided it was time to put me in charge of more. It was worth the wait.

JOURNAL: What has God filled you with a desire to do in service to his kingdom? Write down any ways God has been shaping you to do the work you hope to do. In what small ways can you prove your faithfulness to him while you wait?

_____

_____

_____

_____

_____

_____

_____

_____

_____

_____

_____

_____

_____

_____

_____

_____

_____

38

ADOPT A POSITIVE PERCEPTION OF WOMEN AND HOUSEWORK

> *. . . by love serve one another.*
>
> GALATIANS 5:13

It had been a normal Saturday for me. I enjoyed a relaxing time with Jesus and a cup of coffee during the morning, but then it was time to get to work, starting with Saturday morning waffles. I don't remember when I started the tradition, but for years I've spent part of my Saturday mornings stirring up homemade waffles, cooking bacon, and serving them with a glass of milk. It's been a gathering time that we've all come to love.

Then I made a menu for the week, tidied the house, and set to work getting dinner in the crockpot—cutting, chopping, browning. We go to church on Saturday nights, so we're all starving for dinner when we get home around

8:00 p.m. I put the lid on the crockpot, did the dishes, and cleaned out the refrigerator. I made a list and did my Costco and grocery store run. After years of failing to get dinner on the table, I finally figured out that if I put in the time on the weekend to make a menu for the week and buy all of the groceries, the likelihood of me making a good dinner every night would increase by about 90 percent.

When I got home from shopping, I put the groceries away neatly in the pantry and refrigerator and even prepped some of the veggies for the week.

When I was a young wife and mom, I used to chafe against all of this work. I would often feel resentful and think, "Why do I have to do all of this? Why do I have to clean the house and buy all of the groceries and cook and earn a living and make waffles on Saturday?" It felt like indentured servitude.

I think it was when my dad died and life was chaos that I started to see the joy in everyday work. I grew in my appreciation of life and having the health to fold laundry. I valued the fact that my husband and kids were alive and I could serve them. What a joy it was to serve them! For the first time I saw, in painful contrast, what it looks like when the people who "cause all of the work" aren't with you anymore. I know my mom would give anything just to fold my dad's socks again or make him dinner.

To me, *feminism* is an appreciation for the lives around us and the great gift God has given us to serve the people we love. I didn't understand that during my younger years as a wife and mother. Life is too valuable for me to kick against my work in frustration and ingratitude.

JOURNAL: Where do you see resentment creeping in because of your workload? Imagine if you were to lose one of the precious people in your life. What would you miss most about serving that person in love?

39

ACCEPT WILLINGLY THE STRESS OF YOUR VOCATION

> *. . . shall we receive good at the hand of God, and shall we not receive evil?*
>
> JOB 2:10

If I were to be compensated for every hour that I've spent lying awake worrying about a student, wondering how to get a class to behave, or trying to figure out how to explain a difficult new concept, I could retire and go dip my toes in an ocean somewhere. Is anyone ever prepared for the stress that will be an inevitable part of their job? I remember feeling ecstatic that August day when I went into the school office and signed my teaching contract. My dream job was finally in front of me, and I was immediately itching to get into the classroom to create my own space for learning.

As a new teacher, I had no way of knowing how mentally challenging the work would be. I didn't yet appreciate the complexity of managing all of the materials I needed, plus the constant two-way flow of papers between me and my students. I certainly hadn't thought about my role in helping them mature into productive young adults. There were many days I wanted to throw in the towel, but I had to ask myself Job's question: Am I only willing to accept the good from God and not the hard?

I chafed against all of the challenges in the beginning. For some reason I felt like a victim of the job, and hard things were happening to me. But Job's question from the Scripture quoted at the opening of this devotional came to mind. Was I only willing to accept from the Lord the good and fun parts of my job? Was I unwilling to accept from God's hand any hard parts of the job?

When I signed the contract to be a teacher, none of the stressors were detailed in line items. And if I'm honest, the pay scale didn't include compensation for this hidden stress. It was a rosy contract and an equally rosy salary.

In light of Job's statement, I think work contracts should be revised. At the top of a contract, it should say, "Agreement to do meaningful work." I imagine it would be about 20 pages long, single spaced, detailing not only the joys and perks of the work but also the unfiltered stress of what God would allow in the position.

There would be details about sleepless nights and about the true number of hours it takes to do the job well. The relationship struggles among teacher, students, and parents would be detailed in bullet points. The mental taxation would be demonstrated with graphic neuroscientific data. The heartache of working with broken and fallen people would be spelled out.

If we could see this kind of contract, we would know—really know—what we were getting ourselves into. No more victimhood or feeling sorry for ourselves in our future jobs, because we could look at the signature line and say, "Oh yes, I agreed to all of this good and bad from God's hand. I accepted all of this without reservation." Meaningful work means equally daunting stress and painful, hard days. The word *vocation* means a job of great purpose. It's a job worth signing up for, on the dotted line of a truthful contract. We want to use our brains and our hearts when we head into work every day, so let's agree to receive the bad God allows, along with the perks.

JOURNAL: What is stressful about your vocation?
Write a statement of agreement to accept this stress.

He that loveth his life shall lose it; and he that hateth his life in this world shall keep it unto life eternal.

JOHN 12:25

40

WHEN RELATIONAL PEACE REQUIRES YOU TO BEND

Recently, my family went out for pizza with my niece. She's an incredible dancer and athlete who likely could have progressed to an Olympic-worthy circuit in gymnastics. Her parents weren't comfortable with all that path required, so she's now on a dance team at her school, where she can still make use of her amazing skills. At dinner we talked about flexibility and the ability to do heel kicks—the kind where your knee touches your nose. My niece can do those. She also shared with us a video of a young woman who could stand flat on one foot and move her other leg to match the hour hands on a clock, all the way from the 6 o'clock position around to the 4 o'clock position. It was impressive, but also painful to watch.

In the past, the Lord has asked me to bend about that far in some of my relationships, and I want to tell you that it hurts. Sometimes, to keep peace in a challenging relationship, he has required me to stretch myself to a place where I feel pain and might simply break. God expects us to die to ourselves in this world. There's no sugarcoating this. If we want to have eternal life, we have to be willing to give up what we want our lives to be in this world. We often have to be the ones who bend. We have to be the ones who sacrifice. We have to be the ones who think of what the other person needs instead of what we want.

God also shows us if we're loving a *thing* in our lives more than a person. I've been in that place, demanding a right or a privilege about a *thing* I desired. I've seen my inner self screaming a childish demand about the life I thought I should have. There are things I've had to give up for the sake of good relationships—oh, how I loved those things. I have wept for them like a toddler who had a favorite toy ripped from her hand.

Also, I've had to state loudly what I *will* love. I will love God with all of my heart. I love to be obedient to him. I also love my life too much to give up eternity for the temporary desires in front of me right now. But I am also a human being, and I have emotions that swirl around my desire to be obedient, so I have brought the decision to lose my life and all my feelings about dying to myself to the Lord. I have learned to ask him to help me bend well.

JOURNAL: Where do you need to bend to preserve a relationship? What do you love that you hate to give up in order to do this?

_____

_____

_____

_____

_____

_____

_____

_____

_____

_____

_____

_____

_____

_____

_____

_____

41

SURVIVING THE SMALL BUT PAINFUL FAILS OF LIFE

> *A merry heart doeth good like a medicine: but a broken spirit drieth the bones.*
>
> PROVERBS 17:22

We were treating my son, Caleb, and daughter-in-law, Mallory, to burritos one afternoon, when my son told us about a great meal of tacos his new bride lovingly made for him earlier that week. He had just fixed his plate in the kitchen and turned to sit down in the living room when he promptly spilled the entire plate of food.

Mallory told us that Caleb quickly grabbed a spatula, scooped all of the taco fixings back onto his plate, and proceeded to eat it all. She tried to get him to stop, but he wanted to honor her hard work. When we stopped laughing, I couldn't help but say, "Ah, this is the stuff good marriages are made of."

It reminded me of the day I worked so hard to make a meal from scratch, including homemade mashed potatoes, for my young family of four. My culinary skills and self-discipline in the kitchen were lacking in those early years, so it was a big deal that I had peeled potatoes, let alone cut them up, cooked them, and mashed them with butter, milk, and salt.

With my family around the table, I proudly carried the bowl over, only to lose my grip and have it drop, upside down, on our kitchen floor. I stared at the mess and then looked up at my husband and two kids. Everyone was holding their breath, waiting to see what kind of emotional storm the potato disaster was going to kick up. I wanted to cry, but when I saw their faces, I made a sad little laugh instead.

I think sometimes it's easier to face a big crisis than it is to face all of those little fails that happen in a day. These types of small spills sometimes chip away at my hope. Hardly a day goes by without some kind of mishap that could have been avoided with one breath more of care. The shame of mistakes is painful to me, especially since I am a woman who wants to live well, care for people, and work with excellence. Each little error makes me wonder if I'm ever going to get it all right.

A cheerful heart does good in a time of failure, even a small one. I think a merry heart knows how to laugh and turn failure into a funny story. When I chose to laugh at my sad bowl of potatoes ruined on the floor, it worked like a kind of medicine for me and my family. We did not suffer for lack of potatoes, and the cheerful outlook on my mistake allowed joy to reign, instead of a crushed spirit. We live in a broken world, and we feel it in all of the small mistakes we make in a week. One remedy is to develop a ready sense of humor and employ it often.

JOURNAL: Describe the last "dumb" mistake you made and were able to laugh about. How did your cheerful sense of humor redeem the painful moment?

42

MAKE ROOM FOR SOME NATURAL DOWN TIMES IN LIFE

> *But he himself went a day's journey into the wilderness, and came and sat down under a juniper tree: and he requested for himself that he might die . . .*
>
> **1 KINGS 19:4**

For our fifteenth wedding anniversary, our church gave Matt and me a trip. We boarded a plane and arrived in central Texas, where we stayed in an Airbnb that boasted a spectacular view of nature rimmed by city lights in the background. We spent hours just looking outside and watching the sky and the birds. I felt all of the meetings, deadlines, and demands slip away, and it felt really good.

Then a few days in, I started to feel restless, bored, and down. For a few months, I had longed for this break from all of the pressing work I had been doing, but instead I felt almost depressed. Soon I recognized it was the natural physical and mental letdown after a very stressful season. I've learned over the years that I need to budget for downtime after every intense season of life. When we push and push for weeks or even months, there has to be a time when our adrenal systems get some days off, when we can let the mental and physical fatigue melt away. This requires a normal deflation in emotion.

One of my favorite stories in the Bible, of Elijah, tells a similar story. When my husband and I toured Israel a few years ago, we got to stand where Elijah went head-to-head with prophets of Baal and God worked an amazing miracle for the people to see. But after that incredible experience, Elijah was toast. He ran away, reclined under a tree, and told God that he wanted to die. God's answer was to give Elijah a long time to sleep and eat. After that, Elijah was able to get up and get to living again. I find the story of Elijah to be a wonderful example of how we naturally crash after big seasons of exposure, high adrenaline, and expenditure of relational energy.

I accepted the feeling of being down as a sign that I needed rest. Matt needed this kind of rest, too, so one day we slept in and then watched *Fixer Upper* reruns until it was almost time for lunch. A lazy morning and then an afternoon of disc golf in the sunshine was medicine to our weary minds and bodies. The feeling of being down slipped away during the week, and I soon felt ready to jump back into life again. It's good to let our bodies and minds tell us we need to rest.

How do you feel when you stop moving and laboring after a hard season? Describe a time when you allowed yourself to feel down and slow down, and it was just what you needed to be able to keep going again.

_____

_____

_____

_____

_____

_____

_____

_____

_____

_____

_____

_____

43

LIVE IN THE WORLD OF APPRECIATION INSTEAD OF ENVY

> *Wrath is cruel, and anger is outrageous;*
> *but who is able to stand before envy?*
>
> **PROVERBS 27:4**

Recently, my tourist dream of a lifetime came true, and I finally got to go see Magnolia Silos in Waco, Texas. We had watched the show *Fixer Upper* for years, and I was enthralled by the entrepreneurial spirit of Chip and Joanna Gaines, by Joanna's impeccable taste in decorating, and by the quality of the couple's work ethic. I wanted to see, in person, what I had watched them create on television. For weeks before our vacation, Matt talked about how fun it would be to see our "friends" Chip and Joanna when we got to Texas. When we pulled up to the side street and parked, I felt like I did at the entrance of

Disneyland for the first time. No joke. There were the silos! Just like on television.

On Instagram, I'd been watching Joanna Gaines put the finishing touches on Magnolia Press, the new coffee shop around the corner from the silos, which opened the week before we got there. And here I was, in line, waiting to say my order. While I was taking it all in, I started to get a strange feeling. It was a combination of smallness and plain old envy. Everything Joanna does is beautiful and perfect. In that moment, it seemed like all she has to do is imagine something, and it magically comes into existence. As we walked through the Magnolia complex, with our rich coffees in hand, that nagging feeling continued: "Why is everything Joanna does perfect and big and lovely, and who am I? Why isn't my life like hers?"

Sometimes when one woman does something well, it presents some kind of painful thorn that pokes at our hearts from underneath and causes envy. I'm aware of this tactic of holding up another woman in comparison, so I bowed out. I refused to go there. I spoke words of truth to my own soul.

Joanna Gaines has incredible gifts, but the God who created me did not make me like her and did not give me her gifts. Instead of going down the road of envy, I turned my feelings into a prayer for my own life, and these words felt good and admirable. "Lord," I said, "I want to use the gifts you've given me with as much energy and with as much excellence as Joanna Gaines uses hers. You've made me to write and teach and lead in women's ministry, and I pray you will help me have the same work ethic and creativity that are evidenced here at the silos today."

Instead of sitting in a seat of envy toward Joanna Gaines, I chose to look up to her and be inspired by the qualities she possesses that I can emulate in the places where I work with my own mind and heart and hands. I chose to rejoice in her success. God has blessed the work of her hands, and I celebrated this for her. I refused to let the ugliness of envy taint and spoil the beauty of what she had worked so hard to build.

As women, we have a responsibility to celebrate one another, be inspired by one another, and steer clear of being envious of one another.

JOURNAL: What woman do you feel tempted to be envious of because of her life and success? Write down the character qualities in her that you admire, and write a prayer asking God to help you grow in those qualities.

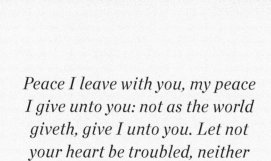

*Peace I leave with you, my peace
I give unto you: not as the world
giveth, give I unto you. Let not
your heart be troubled, neither
let it be afraid.*

JOHN 14:27

44

KNOW HOW TO HAVE PEACE WHEN IT SEEMS LIKE NO ONE ELSE DOES

On a recent Saturday afternoon, I went to do my normal grocery shopping, and I started at Costco. For the first time ever, where there should have been ground beef there was an entire empty refrigerator section. The store was brighter, because most of the upper shelves were empty and the light was shining through them. When I paid for my food and left the store, I walked past the food court, where all of the tables had been removed so that no one could eat there. Fear and panic because of a world-wide virus had created empty shelves, while the newly required social distancing measures had put an end to the enjoyment of sitting down to a good hot dog or slice of pizza with family.

On Sunday night the email came in: School would be closed down because of the coronavirus. We had been watching the growing pandemic in the world around us, but the effects were arriving late, as everything else seems to do, to our little corner of Montana. And to think that just two months prior to this, I had been trying not to freak out about getting the flu while I had so much responsibility on my plate. I had no idea that the flu would seem like child's play in just a short time.

On Monday morning, I woke up and went to an all-faculty meeting at school, where we were made to sit with a chair between each of us. There we discussed how we would completely change our teaching style, from classroom instruction to online learning. Somehow, we were supposed to keep personal contact with our students, explain new concepts, send out homework, and figure out how to assess kids from a distance. It was overwhelming.

But before we talked through what online teaching would look like, we did something else. Our superintendent opened his Bible and read about how God takes care of us. Then we all stood and sang the hymn "It Is Well with My Soul." Stress and worry dissipated as we sang about the fact that Jesus has shed his own blood for our souls.

Jesus's words have been a comfort to me in this trial. He says he has left peace for us, and he says that peace isn't like what the world offers.

When fear bubbles up, I am singing again, "It is well with my soul." I am reading the precious promises of God's care in the Bible. I am leaning hard on the Lord, looking for peace only in him.

JOURNAL: What is troubling your heart right now, causing you to be afraid? Describe what you will do mentally to seek peace from Jesus.

_____

_____

_____

_____

_____

_____

_____

_____

_____

_____

_____

_____

_____

_____

_____

_____

_____

45

IT'S NEVER TOO LATE TO MAKE GOOD MONEY DECISIONS

> *. . . for with God all things are possible.*
>
> MARK 10:27

Matt doesn't know this, but I've been squirreling away money toward one of our financial goals. I manage our finances and have been working on this project for almost a year. Lord willing, in a few months I'm going to be able to announce to him that we have enough money tucked away to cover our expenses for three months, as an emergency fund. I can hardly wait to see the look on his face, and I've been daydreaming about how I'll give him the news.

I never thought we'd get to this place financially. In our early years of marriage, we struggled to pay thousands of dollars' worth of college debt. I was a stay-at-home mom, and Matt was working in the mental health field, earning far less than he was worth. We could barely pay bills, and the extras we needed came from generous parents. They were so kind. Even so, I cried over the checkbook every month and begged God to help us get out of debt so that we could start funding our own life. Those were the days when I was grateful for hand-me-down clothing and hand-me-down vehicles, and for Mom and Dad coming to visit and buying groceries. It seemed we would never dig our way out of debt and definitely never move forward financially.

During that time, I worked desperately toward our first financial goal: to get $1000 in emergency savings. When you're living hand-to-mouth, the thought of having an extra thousand dollars seems laughable. I was able to tuck away $5 here and $10 there. One day I saw that my secret stash had three zeros on the end, the amount I had been praying for in our checking account. This meant no more turning to a credit card when something unexpected happened. We could borrow that money for emergencies from ourselves. What seemed like an impossible financial goal for us was not impossible for God. That thousand dollars changed everything.

One decade after Matt had graduated with his master's degree, we asked our friends to walk with us to our mailbox, which is across the street. They looked at us like we were a little crazy. When we got there, I held up our final college loan payment and, with great ceremony, put it into the mail slot. We returned to the house, and I poured sparkling cider for all of us in celebration. No debt. That seemed like reaching for the moon, but by God's grace we did it.

We're now in our fifties, and it feels like our finances over the years have been three steps forward and two steps back. For the last several years, every time I've tried to put some money toward our third financial goal, some unforeseen expense has come up. I've struggled not to lose hope. In spite of this, I am about to tell my husband that we have done it. This goal was to get three months of salary in emergency savings so that if one of us were to lose our jobs, we would have three months of wiggle room to survive without a paycheck. I can't believe we're just a few months away from this being a reality, and again I see that with God's help anything is possible.

The next stop is retirement. I've joked that we'll be able to retire at noon on the day we die, because that's when we'll finally have money. But I shouldn't laugh. It's wise to plan for the future, and God honors the wise desires of our hearts. He is able to make anything possible, and I certainly am a witness of this. So, I tell you not to despair. Don't give up! It's not too late for you to start making wise money decisions and doing your best to move toward them, even if at present you're in a bad place because of the pandemic and the world economy. Even now, you can ask God to help you.

JOURNAL: Describe your financial status right now. What financial goals do you have, and how are these in line with God's wisdom about money?

_____

_____

_____

_____

_____

_____

_____

_____

_____

_____

_____

_____

_____

_____

_____

_____

_____

_____

_____

46

HOW TO HANDLE THE SORROW OF LIVING FAR FROM FAMILY

> *I will offer to thee the sacrifice of thanksgiving, and will call upon the name of the LORD.*
>
> **PSALM 116:17**

It was a perfect day in Texas in February. It was several days after we had visited Magnolia and the silos, with bright sun, no humidity, and a slight cool breeze. Matt and I were enjoying the respite from our eternal winter in Montana, with cloudy days, snow on the ground, and icy winds. It was the last day of our trip, and my husband and son were playing disc golf—a fun way to spend a vacation day with Caleb, who had moved to Texas with his wife. It was my job to be impressed with how amazing they were—regardless of how they were actually playing.

Now that Caleb was out of school, married, and working, he had only two weeks of vacation. We would soon go back to weekly FaceTime conversations and long-distance living, seeing Caleb and Mallory maybe once a year. My mother's heart squeezed with a familiar pain.

Over 30 years ago I went to the same central Texas college where we sent our son. Back then my parents and I had limited conversations because we had to pay for every minute. There was no such thing as face-to-face calling over the Internet. I met a Montana guy at school. We got married and moved to the northwesternmost corner of his home state.

For three decades, I've traveled 12 hours by car, over two dangerous mountain passes, to visit my parents in Wyoming. All I've known in my married life has been a long-distance relationship with my parents. They only saw their grandkids a few times a year. Every other Christmas has been spent at my folks' house, and only occasionally did they ever come our direction.

Living far away never stops hurting.

I've learned to manage this deep pain of separation over the years by defaulting to thankfulness. I can either sit and mourn and be miserable in the goodbye, or I can be thankful for how much it hurts. The remedy for my squeezing heart is to rejoice at how much I love my family. Thank God it's painful to leave! Thank God for the tears we all drip when we say goodbye. Thank God for the tight hugs that get repeated with everyone two or three times. Thank God we make plans and look forward to the next time we'll see each other.

I am rich in family.

So, I'll hug my son goodbye, and Matt and I will drive to the airport. It will cut my mother's heart to walk away from him. But after I shed a few tears, I will turn to thankfulness and let the sweet love and enjoyment of my son and his wife wash over my bleeding heart.

JOURNAL: What pain of separation have you experienced in life? Write ways you are thankful for the people you miss.

_____

_____

_____

_____

_____

_____

_____

_____

_____

_____

47

HOW DO YOU RESPOND WHEN YOUR COWORKERS ARE JERKS?

> *Not rendering evil for evil, or railing for railing: but contrariwise blessing; knowing that ye are thereunto called, that ye should inherit a blessing.*
>
> **1 PETER 3:9**

A while ago I was talking to a young woman with whom I am friends. She was in her first job out of college. It was a challenging social work job with special-needs children. She was learning how to respond to children who would kick, hit, spit, and throw things at her. It was physical, exhausting work. When I asked her how work was going, she said she couldn't wait to get a new job. But the reason wasn't because of the kids; it was because of her horrible coworkers.

She said some of the coworkers regularly call out what she does wrong on the job and then turn around and tell her boss. Sometimes they lie. She said her supervisor doesn't seem to like her but loves to gossip about drama at work, so the behavior of her coworkers isn't reprimanded but is almost welcomed. Three of her friends had quit because they couldn't take the work environment anymore. We both agreed the behavior of her coworkers was terrible and unprofessional. I asked her how she handled such childish behavior on a daily basis. One of her fellow coworkers, who loves Jesus, encouraged her to always do good, so this young woman was learning to stick up for herself and not return the evil that was being served to her.

"Really I'm learning to tame my tongue," she told me. "I'm not a doormat. If someone accuses me of doing something wrong, I calmly explain that I'm doing what I've been taught, but then I try to divert my attention to one of our clients. Instead of saying something I regret, I turn my attention to play with a child."

Her goal is to give her coworkers no reason to find fault with her. When she's finished with the therapy room, she makes sure every item is put away and all of the surfaces are clean. She also has determined to do every task to the best of her ability for God to see. I was impressed at her decision to respond well to her hard work environment instead of looking for a way to repay how she was treated.

JOURNAL: Who in your life treats you in an evil way? What is your typical response? What would it look like to respond to that person with good instead of evil?

Be ye angry, and sin not . . .

EPHESIANS 4:26

48

DON'T LET ANGER BE AN EXCUSE TO DO WHAT IS WRONG

I zipped up my down coat when I got out to put gas in my car, as an icy wind had slipped over the Canadian border. While waiting for my receipt to print, I saw a woman pull up to the gas pumps, get out of her truck, slam the door, and walk toward a man who had just parked. She was pointing her finger and screaming at him, telling him he needed to learn how to drive. Her rant included the F-word about five times. There were others at the gas pumps, and we all stood there with wide eyes. Her fierce anger scorched not only the offending driver, but also all of us within a 200-yard radius of the gas pumps.

In my classroom I have a sign that explains to students my three core values. The first of these is "use good language." I have an English degree, and I'm a Spanish teacher. When I use the term "good language," I mean proper grammar and good sentence construction, but I also mean good language in quality of word choice. In my classroom, words and phrases like "idiot," "shut up," and "I hate you" are forbidden. These common words and phrases may seem benign, but they can be delivered in just as scathing a tone as the "bad" cuss words.

Even though I teach at a private Christian school, my experience has been that students don't always use good language when speaking of themselves and when communicating with each other.

I'm constantly asking my students, in a firm but gentle tone, to speak kindly to one another. My own kids went to public school, and I fear to know how many times they heard the F-word and the S-word in a single day. All I had to do was stand in the high school hallway for five minutes to hear them several times myself.

God is a God of language—he created the entire world by the spoken word—and he is good and kind. In turn, our language should be good and kind, even if an injustice has been done to us. We can be angry or frustrated, but it's wrong to let that anger color our speech into something dark and abusive. Paul tells the followers of Jesus that it's okay to be angry. If another driver cuts you off, you have a right to be angry, but you don't have permission to sin.

With my car fueled and my heart wounded, I drove the 10 minutes to school. As I was driving, I started to think about women, particularly those who spend an exorbitant amount of money to make themselves look young and beautiful. But one of the best investments we can make is to use good, uplifting language as a matter of habit, even when we're angry. The behavior of the woman at the gas station was ugly, and I didn't even notice what she looked like on the outside. Controlling our words and tone of voice when we're angry is the truest beauty product in which we can invest.

JOURNAL: What ugly language comes out of your mouth when you're angry? (Go ahead and write down these words. See how ugly they are on paper.) Think of a woman you know who is patient and kind, even when she is angry. Write down what you admire about her responses to anger.

49

DON'T GIVE UP ON THE GOOD WORK YOU DO

> *And let us not be weary in well doing: for in due season we shall reap, if we faint not.*
>
> GALATIANS 6:9

As I've mentioned previously, I recently began my job as women's ministry director at our church. Four months prior to that, I assembled a team of more than a dozen women. Some of them came and went as we went through the planning. I had to figure out how to communicate my vision for the ministry and get it into some kind of work-able format. It also meant months of firsts for me: first time figuring out the chains of command at church, first time submitting a budget to the church, first time leading plan-ning meetings for multiple events, and first time setting up our social media platforms to get the word out about what we were doing. It was exhausting, and all of the new came with a peppering of small fails.

This year also found me responsible for teaching a class of 26 freshmen. They wouldn't fit in my tiny classroom, so I had to figure out how to organize and cart my teaching materials to the farthest end of the building every day to a borrowed classroom that would accommodate my class. It meant learning to share a space with another teacher and to manage too many freshmen who had a lot of maturing to do.

I also teach a 25-minute Bible lesson to several dozen third- and fourth-graders at church every week. I love this job, but one night, after a long day of school and nearing the end of my writing contract, I plopped down on the couch in my husband's office at church. "I'm just tired," I said. "I want to be done with school and women's ministry and writing and teaching children."

Despite my fatigue, I walked into the room full of children and taught them the good news of Jesus. When I was done, I asked those who wanted to put their faith in Jesus to raise their hand. One little girl did, and I helped her pray. Together we prayed our belief that Jesus came to earth, died, then came back to life—all to rescue us from our sins. She ended by naming Jesus as Lord of her life. It was a blessed moment.

Paul tells the followers of Jesus not to get tired of doing good, because eventually it's going to pay off. Well, it really paid off that night for that little girl, I can tell you. She entered into the kingdom of God. If I had caved to my fatigue, that might not have happened. God puts a lot of good work in front of us, and we're going to have days when it's exhausting. We have to keep going, though. It's always worth it.

JOURNAL: What good work has God given you to do that is making you feel bone tired? Write a prayer of determination, committing yourself to keep going in the work.

_____

_____

_____

_____

_____

_____

_____

_____

_____

_____

_____

_____

_____

_____

50

AVOID THE CONSTANT TEMPTATION TO BE A SLACKER

> *He also that is slothful in his work is brother to him that is a great waster.*
>
> **PROVERBS 18:9**

Each school year we have 10 days when students attend seminars instead of regular classes. Each grade level spends the days working on one specific topic of study, such as creating a mock trial. Because I'm a part-time teacher, I don't run any seminars. I still work during classroom hours but don't have students to teach.

Those two weeks are wonderful for me. I use the precious time to plan and prepare for the upcoming weeks. I'll admit, being a teacher without a class full of students is so much easier. I sit down at my desk for four hours a day and walk through lesson plans, rethinking and tweaking ideas. I add in a few new creative elements, create online games, and write tests. It feels so good to add all that preparation to my three-ring lesson plan binders.

But it can also be really tedious. My eyes get tired and my neck gets stiff from staring at the computer for hours. I sometimes find myself weary, and I start to become extremely creative at finding ways not to sit at my desk. I often get up to look at the little kids playing on the playground. I have a snack, then I think about lunch. I have an extra-long chat with the school secretary when I pick up copies from the school printer. One day, I confessed to her that I was feeling a little lazy and avoiding work.

"I think I need a mom to say to me, 'Remember you came here to work,'" I said, half hoping she'd be the one to say it.

I thought about my freshman class. It seemed to have a large number of students who lacked discipline. I was imagining what would happen in the classroom if I were to give them work and then leave the room. Many of them would be out of their desks, talking, or throwing things to each other. There was no way this class had the self-discipline to work if I weren't watching them.

There I was, looking at lesson plans, shaking my head at those unruly students, when the Lord told me that I wasn't doing a whole lot better at being self-disciplined than my current freshman class. No one was watching me work that week. All of the teachers and students and the principal were in the other building, busy with seminars, and not a soul was keeping track of what I was accomplishing.

I felt a renewed sense of responsibility, as I judged my own work habits and built up a determination to focus and be responsible for using my time well, even though only God saw whether I was being slothful or hardworking. I wanted to be trustworthy to use the time the way I was supposed to be using it.

JOURNAL: When you work unsupervised, would you describe yourself as procrastinating and slothful or responsible and hardworking? What motivates you to work hard even when no one is watching?

51

GO TO THE ONE WHO RECEIVES YOU JUST AS YOU ARE

> *Wherefore receive ye one another, as Christ also received us to the glory of God.*
>
> **ROMANS 15:7**

We spent a week visiting our old stomping grounds in central Texas, and that meant a few trips to visit our alma mater, the University of Mary Hardin-Baylor (UMHB) in Belton. It's a beautiful, historic campus, and it's where I met my husband and got my degree. It's the place where I learned how to live away from home, to endure a new climate, and to adapt to a very different culture from the one in Wyoming where I had grown up.

UMHB is the place where we made some of our closest, lifelong friends. We met the university vice president and his wife for lunch, but I only saw them as sweet old friends. He was the one who cheated at cards with my husband and made us laugh until our stomachs hurt. She was the one with whom I walked through my first pregnancy. The day my daughter was born, she visited me in the hospital, only for her own water to break and her son to be born. We shared a hospital room together with our newborns that night. The friends we made at school are people with whom we've walked through difficult things. We've annoyed each other and offended each other at times, but the love has stayed strong. We've watched each other grow as adults and servants of the Lord.

As we met up with various old friends, I was reminded of flaws and faults in each. Somehow these made the friends more comfortable and real in my mind. But this also acted as a mirror on myself, reminding me that I, too, have flaws and faults. I wondered if, when my old friends saw me after so many years, they would only think of my past failures. This idea made a sense of shame wash over me as I recalled so many selfish and unkind things I had done in the past. I became acutely aware of my own short-comings as a human being.

In different encounters with each old school friend, I felt uncomfortably self-conscious and wondered what my friends held in their memories of me. What personality traits drove them nuts when we were younger? What offenses did my appearance bring up in the minds of my friends, and was there any pain in seeing me? Thankfully, with each encounter I received a warm reception. We hugged and reminisced and talked about our lives. There was no room for shame to grow as I received my old friends, faults and all, and they lovingly received me, faults and all.

My thoughts went to Jesus. He has accepted me. He has called me a friend, and he didn't wait until I was flawless to do it. Certainly, he is working to help me mature on the inside, but I can always think of his love for me and feel known and completely welcome. I don't feel afraid that someday I'm going to act in such a way that he's going to throw up his hands and give up on me. He's a friend who is safe. He stays.

JOURNAL: In what relationships do you tend to feel a sense of shame, like you're just not a good person and maybe aren't accepted? Describe the acceptance you've discovered in your relationship with Jesus.

Rejoice with them that do rejoice, and weep with them that weep.

ROMANS 12:15

52

ACCEPT THE PAIN
THAT COMES WITH A
COMPASSIONATE HEART

They called us *mzungu*. Little kids shouted it into our van
windows as we drove by, and we learned it was the term
used in Uganda to refer to rich, white foreigners. In that
third-world country, they spoke from their poverty. It was
my first experience going to a country where people
worked from morning until late at night to make enough
money to buy food for the day. I wasn't a rich person in the
United States by any means, but in Kampala I could feel
my comparative wealth, and it pained me.

One afternoon we were driving through the city, and we
came into a horrible traffic jam of cars, trucks, motorcycles,
and cows. It slowed us down considerably, and I could feel
the press of the other vehicles just inches from our own. It
was then that I looked out of my window and saw a man
on a bicycle trying to ride between us and another vehicle.
The other driver didn't see him and came in close, crushing the front of the bicycle.

We all watched the man get up and push his destroyed bicycle off to the side of the road, where he sat down in complete despair. His body was fine, but I could tell his transportation and livelihood most likely had just been demolished.

"Now see?" our driver said. "That was his fault!"

In Uganda, the cars have the right-of-way, and pedestrians and bicycles do not. If someone gets hit by a car, it's not the fault of the driver of the car. I understand that, according to Ugandan law, this man was to blame for what happened to his bicycle, but all I could see was his defeated slump to the ground, his shoulders dropped in hopelessness, and his face that told me how devastating the accident had been to his entire way of life.

The moment passed but my memory of that incident remains. Often something will trigger my mind to go back to that day in traffic, and I can feel the man's pain all over again. In my heart, a hundred times over the last decade since my trip to Uganda, I've cried out to this man, "I'm sorry! I'm sorry about your bike. I'm sorry everyone says it's your fault. I'm sorry this *mzungu* couldn't get money to you that day, to be of help in your time of need."

I am called to feel the pain of others, to cry with them when they cry. It is not pleasant, but this is the life of the tender, compassionate heart Jesus desires us to have. From this feeling comes a desire to help. From the pain comes action. I couldn't help the man on the side of the road that day in Uganda, but I can help others in similar circumstances.

JOURNAL: Write about the last time you wept with someone who was weeping. What action did that deep compassion lead you to take to bring help and relief to the person?

_____

_____

_____

_____

_____

_____

_____

_____

_____

_____

_____

_____

_____

_____

_____

_____

_____

INDEX

H

habits, 103, 177
health
   provisions for, 8-10
honest/honesty, 81, 103, 118,
      126, 137. *See also*
      Psalm 139:14
humble/humility, 66, 82, 85.
      See also James 4:6

J

James 1:2-4
   journal entry, 15
   joyful, as response to
      stress, 12-15
James 1:5
   journal entry, 116
   wisdom, in troubling
      situations, 114-116
James 1:19
   anger, slow to, 92-94
   journal entry, 95
James 4:6
   humility, 82-85
   journal entry, 85
Jeremiah 29:13
   journal entry, 57
   trust, 55-57
Job 1:20
   journal entry, 18
   worship, 16-17
Job 2:10
   acceptance, of hardships,
      136-138
   journal entry, 139

John 12:25
   journal entry, 143
   sacrifice, 141-142
John 14:27
   journal entry, 157
   peace, 154-156
joyful, 115. *See also*
      James 1:2-4

K

kindness, 52, 81. *See also*
      Ephesians 4:32

L

Luke 6:29
   journal entry, 53
   unfairness, 51-52
Luke 12:23
   abundance, of life, 8-10
   journal entry, 10

M

Mark 10:27
   financial success, 158-160
   journal entry, 161
Matthew 5:14
   darkness, be the
      light in, 19-21
   journal entry, 21
Matthew 6:19
   coveting, as possessions,
      121-122
   journal entry, 123
Matthew 6:27
   journal entry, 49
   worry, no gain from, 47-49

R

redeem/redeeming, 26–27
refuge. *See* Psalm 46:1
rejoice, 119, 152, 163.
    See also Philippians
    4:4; Romans 12:15
responsibility
  overwhelming, can be, 13
  personal, for self, 2
rest/rejuvenation, 28, 67,
    107–108. *See also*
    1 Kings 19:4
Revelation 22:13
  children, prayer for, 23–24
  journal entry, 25
Romans 8:28
  faith, as complete, 65–67
  journal entry, 67
Romans 12:2
  journal entry, 36
  obedience, through
    prayer, 33–35
Romans 12:15
  empathy, 182–184
  journal entry, 185
Romans 15:7
  acceptance, of others,
    178–180
  journal entry, 181

S

Sabbath. *See* Genesis 2:3
sacrifice, 5–6, 162. *See also*
    John 12:25; Matthew 16:25
salvation. *See* Colossians 3:3
save/saving, 104

service, 105, 118–119. *See also*
    Galatians 5:13
strength, 14, 28, 85, 86.
    See also Psalm 46:1
stress/stressful
  time/season, 13–14, 90, 148.
    See also Matthew 6:34
  work place, 84, 136–138,
    156, 166
suffer/suffering
  comfort comes from, 9–10
  joy in, look for, 12, 17, 146

T

temptation
  proving, as one's self, 14
thankful/thankfulness, 32, 48,
    52, 102. *See also*
    Psalm 116:17;
    1 Thessalonians 5:18
timing
  Gods, 5
tolerance
  coworkers, of, 165–166
tongue
  taming, response, 166
trust/trusting
  unquestioning, 14–15, 24,
    28, 67, 105. *See also*
    Jeremiah 29:13
trustworthy, 177

U

understanding, gaining, 1, 2
unfairness. *See* Luke 6:29
unworthiness, 62, 118, 119

W

willingness
  for learning, 1-3
wisdom, gaining, 1-2,
      71, 114-116, 161.
      See also Ephesians
      5:15-16; James 1:5

worry, 9, 14, 24-25, 91, 136,
      156. *See also* Matthew
      6:27; 1 Peter 5:7
worship, 5, 24, 27-28, 66-67.
      See also Job 1:20
worth/worthy, 6, 131, 138,
      141, 174. *See also*
      Ephesians 3:8

REFERENCES

Chesterton, G. K. *The Collected Works of G.K. Chesterton*. Vol. 1. San Francisco, CA: Ignatius Press, 1986.

King James Bible (BlueLetterBible.org).

Rauschenbusch, Walter. "The Little Gate to God." In *The Pilgrim Hymnal*, edited by Sidney A. Weston. Rev. ed. Boston: Pilgrim Press, 1935.

Thompson, Curt. *The Soul of Shame: Retelling the Stories We Believe about Ourselves*. Downers Grove, IL: InterVarsity Press, 2015.

ABOUT THE AUTHOR

 **Christy Fitzwater** is a writer, high school Spanish teacher, and pastor's wife living in Kalispell, Montana. She is the mother of two adult kids, who are both married. Christy finds it most romantic to serve alongside her preacher husband at church, where they both disciple their church family from different directions. Christy writes small-group Bible-study guides and is the women's ministry director at her church. She has a desire to help women know God and be equipped to live the big and meaningful life he has planned for them. Christy has written three books: *Blameless: Living a Life Free from Guilt and Shame*, *My Father's Hands: 52 Reasons to Trust God with Your Heart*, and *Moving in Close: 52 Bible Study Tips to Help You Know God*. Find more of her devotional writing at christyfitzwater.com.